Topics for Today's Trying Times:

60 Devotionals

By Karen Sachs

Includes Trials, Relationships, Sin, Good & Evil Influences

Topics for Today's Trying Times: 60 Devotionals: Includes Trials, Relationships, Sin, Good & Evil Influences

Printed in the United States of America

ISBN 9798848197587

Distributor: www.amazon.com

The "Content by Title" has a description of the story in the main title and the lesson in the subtitle so that you can find devotionals you have read. Following this is "Content by Subject," and finally "Content by Scripture."

CONTENT BY TITLE

Section 1. The Believer's Relationship with God

v

Section 2. Relying on God in Our Trials

Section 3. Relationships with People

Section 4. Insights on Sin

Section 5. Good and Evil Influences

CONTENT BY SUBJECT

Section 1.
The Believer's Relationship with God

Section 2.
Relying on God in Our Trials

Section 3
Relationships with People

Section 4
Insights on Sin

Section 5
Good and Evil Influences

CONTENT BY SCRIPTURE

ACKNOWLEDGMENTS

At the top of my list of acknowledgements is God as my sufficiency comes from Him. Not just to write, but also physically when I experience complications from my ALS.

God surrounded me with the perfect combination of people to improve on the content of this book and help with my shortcomings. First on that list is Donna Carnahan, not only a friend who I met through Bible study, but also my mentor, teacher, and main editor. As a women's Bible teacher for 50 years, she knows the Bible well and made certain that what you read is doctrinally correct. What an honor to have her by my side. I learned a lot from her, and I hope you do too.

My dear long-time friend Sheri Hanel gave comments and reviewed the book from the standpoint of the reader. If a devotional wasn't encouraging or if it was too preachy, she let me know. In addition to editing, she made suggestions for the artistic aspects of the cover, the drawing, and formatting for the inside of the book.

After Donna's and Sheri's review, Jan Bird, a caring woman who I met at the church library and became a friend, gave her insights. She had a lot to say! What a blessing she is! My cousin, Sue Clark who used to take me to church when I was able to go, gave suggestions for the wording and formatting. All comments resulted in another detailed final review by Donna and me that the others read. After all this, these loving people are still my friends!

Four years ago, I started listening to John Hunt's verse-by-verse Bible teaching when I laid down in the afternoon for pain relief (you can listen to John at www.scripturalinsights.org). When I contacted him through his website to thank him for what he does, he became a friend. He has taught me a lot about the Bible that resulted in some of the devotionals and perseverance to carry out God's will.

Answered prayers from my army of prayer warriors, who love God, resulted in my ALS progressing more slowly than expected, God sustaining and protecting me, and mental clarity, all necessary to finish this book.

MILESTONES

1978 Graduated from high school and started working at Mare Island Naval Shipyard in California

1983 Graduated with a BS degree in Mechanical Engineering; continued working at shipyard

1985 Married Ed Sachs

1994 Shipyard where we worked closed. Ed and I moved to Washington and worked at Puget Sound Naval Shipyard as mechanical engineers

1998 First symptoms of my disease* (see * note at bottom of page)

2006 I became a Christian

2007 Ed diagnosed with brain cancer. I retired on a medical disability at age 46. Ed became a Christian.

2008 April: Because we could no longer care for each other, Ed and I moved to California to live with my mom who accepted us with open arms (my father had died in 2005).

2008 June: Ed died

2008 December: I got my trach and feeding tube

2009 My brother retired and moved in with us so we could care for each other.

2020 My mom died

*My disease has progressed so slowly because it started as a less severe variant, PLS. When it turned to ALS six years ago (in 2016), the doctors predicted it would continue to deteriorate faster than it had been, but slower than typical ALS.

SECTION 1.
THE BELIEVER'S
RELATIONSHIP
WITH GOD

Note: Chapter title on first line describes the story in the first paragraph and subtitle on second line describes the lesson in the second paragraph.

1. A DOG'S HEARING
Faith Comes by Hearing

So then faith comes by hearing,
and hearing by the word of God.
ROMANS 10:17

When my husband and I arrived at his parents for visits, their large dogs excitedly greeted us with wagging tails and licks to our hands. On one visit, I led the way. When they heard our car doors shut, they were let out and came running. At 15 feet away, both dogs froze with an alert stance and perked ears. Why didn't they come with the normal greeting? Finally, I said something. Both dogs relaxed and happily greeted me normally. That day, they relied on their hearing and not sight to recognize me.

Animals and people rely on their senses in various ways. People who lived when the Father sent His Son, Jesus, to be our Savior had the benefit of seeing Jesus. As God and man, Jesus performed miracles to show He was God and produce belief in Him. After Jesus who knew no sin paid the price of death for our sins on the cross, He resurrected on the third day. Thomas didn't believe until he saw the print of the nails on Jesus' hands and side. Like others who saw Jesus' miracles, Thomas' faith was based on sight. Jesus declared that more blessed are those who have not seen and yet have believed (John 20:25-29). Nowadays, we can no longer see Jesus. Becoming a believer starts with a willingness to hear God's word by reading it or someone proclaiming it. God opens the eyes of the unbeliever's spiritually blind heart. They come to God spiritually needy, humble, and mourning over their sin. When they hear the gospel, by God's grace, He gifts them with faith, they repent for their sin, and they become a Christian. Becoming a Christian is called being born again (John 3:7). It is a spiritual birth into our loving God's family where every Christian is our brother or sister in Christ. It isn't our doing, but the work of Christ and God's grace, just as we had nothing to do with our physical birth. Every day, with tears of joy for my salvation and sorrow for what Christ endured to pay for my sins, I thank Him for what He did, and look forward to eternal life in heaven.

 The most valuable words we hear in our lives are those from the word of God.

2. THE WATER SPRING
The Gift of Living Water

"He who believes in Me, as the Scripture has said,
out of his heart will flow rivers of living water."
But this He spoke concerning the Spirit…
JOHN 7:38-39A

On a hike, my husband, Ed, and I ran out of drinking water. We had made it quite far and wanted to go further instead of hiking back to camp but knew it was too dangerous without water. A stream that came down a mountain offered water, but Ed cautioned that animals could have contaminated it. If we could get to its source, it would be safe to drink. We saw what we thought was the source. Could we get to it? Certainly, we had to try. Going off the trail, after a bit of a climb we made our way to the source. It welcomed us gushing directly out of the mountain. With no ponds above it, it was safe to drink. It was so refreshing.

That spring was a gift of nature that gave Ed and me water we desperately needed. We didn't realize there was a different water, spiritual rather than physical, we needed even more. It wasn't until God gave us the gift of faith that we understood what we had been missing. He opened the eyes of our hearts to enlighten us, we repented for our sin, and we became Christians because of our Savior, Jesus. God sent the Holy Spirit, living water, to cleanse us, give us life, and dwell in us. We gained a new nature. He empowered us to overcome sin, gave us the desire to obey God, enabled us to understand the word, and interceded in our prayers. There had been an emptiness in our heart, our soul, we couldn't fill no matter our riches or endeavors. Finally, we were content in our soul. What a pleasant change when we experienced joy, peace, comfort, and guidance from the Holy Spirit. It was superior to what we could find in the world and available whenever we needed it. To top this all off, we looked forward to the promise of eternal life in heaven. It excited us to share about this gift of faith so others could enjoy living water.

 Living water gives us spiritual life while on earth and then eternal life.

3. THE PENDANT
Our Faith in God's Promises

Now faith is the substance of things hoped for,
the evidence of things not seen.
HEBREWS 11:1

I rely on being able to adjust a hospital bed throughout the day and night. When the pendant that controls the bed failed, I had hoped to get a replacement that day as had always been the case in the past. Instead, there was a complication with the contract, and they had to bring a new bed. When I found out they couldn't deliver until the next day, I had mixed emotions of disappointment for the delay; gratitude because the bed failed in the only position where it would be usable; awareness that my situation was bad but could have been serious had my bed failed in a different position; concern for how much increased pain, spasms, and fatigue I would experience from not being able to raise the head of the bed to transfer out of bed; and uneasiness that I wouldn't be able to get out of bed during the night. I succeeded but suffered the physical discomfort that had concerned me.

Our hope that something we desire happens is uncertain and we are often disappointed, but our hope in God's promises is secure and reliable. When we became believers, our faith, a gift from God, took us from doubt to certainty in God's promises we hadn't yet seen or experienced. This is foolish to an unbeliever but makes perfect sense to us. How we live shows our confidence in God. Examples are when, with God's help, we:

- Change our ways to obey God.
- Willingly resist worldly desires.
- Walk in the Spirit rather than fulfilling the lust of our flesh.
- Repent of our sin.
- Receive answers to prayers sent in God's will.
- Trust God's guidance even when it differs from our thoughts or desires.
- Show Christlike love even to those who have hurt us.
- Sense God's joy and peace in our soul when in a trial.

 Actions in our Christian walk reflect our faith in God's promises.

4. PEOPLE BREAK PROMISES, GOD DOESN'T

Counting on God's Promises

And those who know Your name
will put their trust in You;
For You, LORD, have not forsaken
those who seek You.
PSALM 9:10

Even when I had to walk with two canes because of my disease, my husband, Ed, and I seldom needed help around the house. When Ed got cancer, that changed, and we would need a lot of help. It didn't always go as planned. Once, a couple who volunteered to help us promised to come at a certain time. When they didn't come, though disappointed at first, we chose to not bring it up to them and just let it go.

Though people mean well when they make promises, broken promises can be hurtful or harmful. We don't need to concern ourselves about that with God because He always follows through on His promises. Here are a few of God's promises I have experienced.

- *ESCAPE*. God makes a way to escape temptation (1 Cor. 10:13).
- *STRENGTH*. With God strengthening us, we can do all things (Phil. 4:13).
- *FORGIVENESS*. God forgives when we repent (1 John 1:9).
- *DIRECTION*. God directs paths (Prov. 3:5-6).

- *Answered Prayer*. God answers the trusting believer's prayers according to His will (John 15:7).
- *Peace*. Be anxious about nothing, pray about everything, and receive peace beyond human understanding (Phil. 4:6-7).
- *Assurance*. God has not given us a spirit of fear, but of power, love, and a sound mind (2 Tim. 1:7).
- *Understanding*. Jesus understands because He is God-man (Heb. 4:15).
- *Wisdom*. God will provide wisdom without reproach (James 1:5).
- *Hope*. Our God of hope fills us with joy and peace (Rom. 15:13).
- *Stamina*. We won't grow weary (Isa. 40:31).
- *Help*. We can cast our cares on God (1 Pet. 5:7).

 We can always count on God's promises.

5. SMOG
Our Walk Is by Faith, Not Sight

For we walk by faith, not by sight.
2 CORINTHIANS 5:7

When I attended University in Southern California, one of my many new experiences was smog. The air looked dirty, and it smelled. Sunrises and sunsets were red or orange. My skin and hair got dirty faster. A couple of months after my arrival, the first rain came. When I looked outside, I pointed in awe and excitedly exclaimed to my friend, "Look, mountains!" The rain had cleared the smog so we could see the mountains. When I talked to my parents, I was thrilled to share this with them. It was as if I had discovered the mountains, but they had always been there.

After I saw the mountains, I knew they were there even when the smog blocked my view of them. Similarly, Christians don't need to see God to know He is there. Our walk with God is based on faith, not sight. By faith, we believe in our heart what the Bible tells us about living in God's presence. We can experience and recognize God's presence and acts in ways an unbeliever can't. On special occasions, we sense God's presence through the Holy Spirit. We can experience intense emotions stirred by the Holy Spirit when we repent, draw near to God in prayer, get fed thoughts from God's word, or consider God's promises. We experience what the Holy Spirit does when He helps us understand Scripture, produces fruit* in us, or feeds us words when we pray or evangelize. I know God is there because I have experienced all of these and His orchestration of events, protection, strength, sufficiency, joy, and peace that went beyond what I could have done. This is all out of His love for us. So, what does it mean when it seems like God is absent? It doesn't mean God isn't there as He is omnipresent, always everywhere. We sometimes don't detect God when we sin without repenting, aren't in God's will, are disobedient, don't yield control to the Holy Spirit, don't read the Bible, or don't do heartfelt prayer during quality quiet time with God. Other times, God chooses to be silent. He may be testing us. In this case, we haven't done anything wrong. God wants us to walk in faith and not rely on what we sense or experience.

 How ideal heaven will be when we will no longer need to rely on faith because we will finally see God.

*Fruit of the Spirit is love, joy, peace, longsuffering (patience), kindness, goodness, faithfulness, gentleness, and self-control.

SECTION 2.
RELYING ON GOD
IN OUR TRIALS

6. IT IS UP TO GOD
Trials Make Our Faith More Valuable

For You, O God, have tested us;
You have refined us as silver is refined.
PSALM 66:10

My breathing muscles had become so weakened by my disease that I needed a trach connected to a ventilator to keep me alive. Because my disease caused difficulty swallowing food or beverages, the trach might have taken away that ability. So, the doctors planned to surgically install a trach and feeding tube at the same time. I would take in nourishment from a formula through the feeding tube. This was complicated by the fact that most foods made me sick. While in the hospital the evening before the surgery, the doctor shared that he wouldn't install the feeding tube unless the formula I would consume caused no adverse effects. That meant no trach and I would die! This brought shock and fear. To evaluate the formula, the nurse brought two types for me to drink by mouth. Based on their ingredients, it was clear to me that one wouldn't work. If the other one didn't either, I would need to prepare to die. With trust in whatever path God chose for me, I said to myself, "It is up to God." Peace from God filled me. I drank the entire can of formula. After two hours there were no ill effects. I have consumed it every meal for the last 14 years.

The outcome of peace that evening taught me about trust in God for future trials. Trust starts by the gift of faith from God that opens our eyes in belief. God refines our faith to increase our trust when He allows or puts us through trials. In these trials, either we trust God to do His will totally, not at all, or somewhere between. We need to pay attention to the outcome to learn from it. As I experienced that evening, when we trust, we learn how God helps us. When our trust falters, we ask God to show us what we need to do. Increasing our faith in God through trials is like refining silver in the fire where the heat takes the unwanted alloy away leaving the silver purer.

 Trials refine our faith and make it purer and stronger.

7. THE SKILL SAW
God's Abilities

But without faith it is impossible to please Him, for he who comes to God must believe that He is, and that He is a rewarder of those who diligently seek Him.
HEBREWS 11:6

In Washington, my husband and I hired Earl to help us renovate our barn. He had a knack for reinforcing old structures, but not for welcoming women's help. So, I helped the men by handing them what they needed and keeping the work area clean. When another worker didn't show up to cut siding, I retrieved a tiny skill saw and offered my help. Earl laughed at the saw and doubted my abilities. Then, he agreed there was no harm in trying. With Earl and my husband on the scaffolding, Earl called out dimensions. I looked where the siding would go, paying attention to the angles for the eaves and directions of the bevels. After I made the cuts, I tossed the board to Earl. An hour later, the worker showed up. I asked Earl, "Do you want him to take over?" Earl replied, "No, stay where you are and keep doing what you are doing." We agreed to send the worker home. After that day, Earl welcomed me by his side helping with other projects.

Like Earl, we can have doubts about people's abilities until they prove themselves, but we should never have any doubt about God's abilities. God is:

- All-Powerful (Eph. 1:19-21).
- All-Knowing (Psa. 139:1-6).
- Present Everywhere (Psa. 139:7-12).

Though the Bible gives many examples of these, we can still want assurance. God doesn't offer this to unbelievers. As believers, we come to God in faith that He provides. Then in submission to our loving God, we will experience God's power, wisdom, and presence as He chooses to reveal them. I have experienced this many times in my trials when God sustained me beyond what I figured was physically possible in my decrepit body, gave me peace and joy when I shouldn't have had them, and protected me in ways only He could. Also, God has guided me on wonderful paths, and I have sensed His presence. These incredible God-given experiences made trusting Him easier when new trials came my way.

 What a gift when we are allowed to experience God displaying His attributes.

8. PEOPLE'S LIMITED UNDERSTANDING
God's Understanding is Infinite

Great is our Lord, and mighty in power;
His understanding is infinite.
PSALM 147:5

The engineering for critical cleaning processes was one of my responsibilities at my job. For one of the processes, the navy developed a new way to analyze samples. It would save lots of time and money. When I proposed it to my boss, he wouldn't approve it. It was counter to what we had historically done, and he wasn't willing to go against that. Because he knew what he wanted to do, it seemed like he wasn't taking in all the rationale. Without that, he couldn't understand. How frustrating. Confident this was a good approach, I put the rationale in writing so he could take his time studying it and learn all the subtleties. This would give him a better understanding. It worked! He approved it!

To help my boss understand, I had to put the rationale in writing. We never have a concern about God understanding us. There are over 7,000 languages spoken on earth, and God understands them all fluently. God is present everywhere and is all-knowing, which means He knows all our thoughts and our intentions. Then why do we need to pray? Because praying is how we listen as well as speak, seek God and His will, align our thoughts with His, acknowledge Him so He will direct our paths, and thank and praise Him. This builds and deepens our relationship with God. Praying specifically in God's will shows His power when He answers our prayers. When we pray, it isn't important that we deliver exactly the right words, but that we sincerely turn to God. In despair and unable to communicate my needs, I have just said "God please help me" with assurance He knew my needs. If God doesn't answer our prayer right away or how we think He should, it isn't because He didn't understand or hear. It is because He knows what is best, and that may differ from our desire. What a privilege that our loving God understands us so well and answers our prayers.

How amazing that God understands every person even better than they understand themselves.

9. OUTWARD TRAITS WHEN WE PRAY
Disposition of our Hearts When We Pray

Let the words of my mouth
and the meditation of my heart
Be acceptable in Your sight,
O LORD, my strength and my Redeemer.
PSALM 19:14

After my husband, Ed, got cancer, we started going to church and he became a Christian. When Ed prayed, he got on his knees, placed his elbows on the bed, put his hands together flat with fingers facing upward, and bowed his head. Though I knew that the position when praying didn't matter, I said nothing. Where Ed got this idea, I didn't know. It could have been from going to church as a small child. No matter the reason, praying in this position was proper to him to show reverence for God. In Ed's whispers, I could catch a few words. We never prayed aloud to one another, though we admired others who did.

The Bible doesn't specify a proper physical position for prayer. It does give examples of various positions people undertook when they prayed. While neither our outward position when we pray nor our volume matters to God, the inward disposition of our heart does. We are to have a:

- Humble heart that looks up to God and acknowledges He is in control.

- Pure heart that has confessed sin and stands with God.
- Confident heart that knows God hears our prayers.
- Directed heart that prays in God's will.
- Sincere heart that has intellect, emotions, and will surrendered to God.
- Faithful heart that trusts God.

Additionally, when we pray God wants us to seek Him from our heart and not just pray rote words. Praying what we have memorized is alright if it leads us to go deeper with our own words and thoughts. Perfect wording doesn't matter because God knows our hearts. When we pray this way, it can bring heartfelt tears as we commune with God.

 It is our heart that matters most when we pray.

10. THE WINDSTORM
Relying on God, Our Refuge

God is our refuge and strength,
A very present help in trouble.
PSALM 46:1B

After my husband and I moved to Washington, a
windstorm came that was more intense than any we had
ever experienced. As a wind gust approached, it sounded
like a freight train. During the gust, we heard branches
break and thump on the ground. Occasionally, one
landed on our roof. After the gust, it was calm. Then,
another gust approached. Would a tree fall on our house
and harm us? We figured the safest place was in our
house next to our chimney. So, that was where we sat. It
turned out these windstorms occurred a few times each
winter. Getting through the first windstorm gave us
some assurance that a tree was unlikely to fall on our
house. In future windstorms, we didn't stay near our
chimney, but we also didn't wander to the second floor
where there would be more risk. Even so, since we were
relying only on ourselves and not on God, every
windstorm brought fear, worry, anxiety, and uncertainty.

Trials are like the windstorms in that we have no
control over when they will happen, they can cause the
same emotions, and they come and go with varying
intensity. Our house only protected us physically and
with limits. As we experience trials, God will protect us
in ways that go well beyond what anything can do
physically or what we can do for ourselves to address

our undesirable emotions. With God always by our side, in answer to our prayers God will:

- Calm us in our trial or calm our trial.
- Guide us when we don't know which way to go.
- Comfort us and give us peace when emotions overwhelm us.
- Provide a way of escape when tempted.
- Strengthen us when we become weary.

Because I have experienced all of these, I understand how important it is to rely on Him. No way would I want to go through a trial without Him, though it can still be a struggle.

 While we can't control trials, we can control our response by asking for God's help.

11. THE CLIMB
God Gives Us Strength

I can do all things through Christ who strengthens me.
PHILIPPIANS 4:13

Hiking was a favorite activity for my husband, Ed, and me. On one hike, a familiar lake welcomed us with hills on two adjacent sides. A trail we had not spotted before interested us. It went to the top of the hill overlooking the lake. However, it was such a long path we figured we wouldn't have enough time to do it. Instead, we eyed a shortcut up the other hill. It looked steep, but doable. We had enough time to do it and come back the long way. As we headed up it, adrenaline kicked in. There was no stopping us. We got to an almost vertical cliff face. It was much steeper and longer than it looked from the bottom. We made it to a point where we couldn't turn back because it was too steep. Ed warned me, "Don't look down!" What had we gotten ourselves into! Ed confidently leading the way on a path I couldn't have navigated gave me courage that kept me calm. He encouraged me and pulled me up on some sections. I tried my best as I wanted to please him. As we climbed, my strength and skill surprised both of us. At the top, exhilarated and exhausted, we enjoyed a breathtaking view.

Ambition, adrenaline, and Ed's help were key to me conquering the challenge of climbing to the top of the cliff. In life, we face challenges that involve a different climb. They include carrying out God's will, getting through trials, and escaping temptation. God strengthens us in ways that are like what I experienced that day climbing the rocks. With our focus on God, He reveals the path to take and gives us:

- Sufficiency when we lack.
- Guidance to keep us on the right track.
- Motivation to continue forward.
- Courage to persevere.
- Peace beyond our understanding to cope.
- His power that is made perfect in our weakness.
- Stamina when we grow weary.
- Confidence in following God.

The stunning view at the top of the hill is like our new perspective for life when we rely on God to strengthen us. We bless others, succeed in trials, and live righteously.

 God gives us strength for life's challenges when we rely on Him.

12. BROKEN DOWN AND COULDN'T MOVE

God Lifts Us up When Trials Stop Us

The LORD upholds all who fall,
And raises up all who are bowed down.
PSALM 145:14

On a busy freeway with four lanes in each direction, I was driving by myself with no worries on my mind. That changed abruptly when my car broke down. In those days, we didn't have cell phones. Gratefully, there was a rest area half a mile away that I could walk to with no turn offs before or after it for miles. As I approached the phone to call my husband, I dug out coins. What? Where are the slots for the money? Oh my, this isn't a pay phone! I picked up the headset and got a recording that explained about using a calling card. I didn't have such a card! In panic, I hung up. There was no one at the rest stop to ask for help. I listened to the recording again paying attention until the end. It said that in case of difficulties with the calling card, I could talk to an operator. So, I did that with tears of fear not knowing what the operator would do. What a relief when she put the call through to my husband. He arranged for the car to get towed and to get me home.

Just as my broken car couldn't move, we can experience a trial that stops us from progressing in our lives. When we ask, God will lift us up so we can move forward. In contrast to my experience with the phone, God is always easy to reach through prayer. God always hears our prayers, but His answer may not be what we were expecting. We may not have prayed in God's will, it wasn't God's plan, or the timing wasn't right. When He lifts us up, we know it was from Him because we couldn't have done it on our own. This has happened to me many times. Examples include when I struggled with traumatic events, caring for others became exhausting, emotional distress overwhelmed me, or a physical injury, illness, or disease hindered my abilities. In each case, I got to a point where I couldn't handle it. I stopped functioning and melted down. I felt helpless. That changed when I relied on God. He sustained and strengthened me in each of my trials by delivering what I needed. These were such wonderful experiences of God's power, grace, and mercy. Gratefully, I don't suffer as much today because I have learned to reach up to God sooner than I did in my past.

 When we reach up to God, He will lift us up.

13. THUNDERSTORMS
Loving God Brings Calmness in Trials

*"You shall love the LORD your God with all your heart,
with all your soul, and with all your strength."*
DEUTERONOMY 6:5

When my husband and I visited friends in Washington, we camped on their 5-acre property. With so much space, we camped far from their house next to a huge tree. One night when a severe thunderstorm struck, my body trembled with fear. To try to shut it out, I covered my eyes so I wouldn't see the lightning. Covering my ears was futile. Running to the safety of the house would have been too dangerous. Gratefully, the lightning didn't strike us or the tree. When we visited the Grand Canyon, we had a very different experience. After viewing the Canyon, we set up camp about 30 miles away. That night, an impressive thunderstorm struck the Canyon. With an unobstructed view across the desert, we could see frequent lightning strikes, but we couldn't hear the thunder. As we watched from the serenity of our campground, we were so happy we weren't in the storm.

We experienced these thunderstorms in two very different ways. Up close, it was terrifying. Far away, it wasn't a threat and didn't bother us. Just as distance took us from the terror of the thunderstorm to a calm place, loving God can separate us from the turmoil of life's trials. God does this for us when we love Him completely, with our heart, soul, and strength. This is the first and most important commandment. When we follow it, we put our idols and pride aside to put our focus where it needs to be on our loving God. When we love God, we experience His love, guidance, comfort, and protection. This calms our stress and anxiety from trials and brings peace. Moving 30 miles from the thunderstorm brought my husband and me peace, even though the storm was severe. When we go through trials, loving God completely can bring us peace even when the trials are extreme.

 Loving God brings calmness amid turmoil.

14. MY IDOL
Rely on God Rather Than Idols

The righteous cry out, and the LORD hears,
And delivers them out of all their troubles.
PSALM 34:17

Being an engineer meant everything to me. I loved my job. It was my priority. With my job, I had a purpose. Without it, in my mind I was nothing. Gratefully, I was still able to do my job when my disease caused relentless increasing weakness and fatigue. I didn't consider myself handicapped because I could work even though I used two canes. I rationalized that if I could work, my disease must not be that bad. Working kept my focus away from the problems my disease caused. Though I felt good about myself when I worked, doing so was bad as it took a toll on my weakening body for years. I was in denial about the harm working caused and only focused on its pleasures. Another consideration was money. The more money I made, the more I would have to take care of my medical needs after I retired on medical disability. So, I delayed retiring as long as I could, which turned out to be too long and caused sickness the last several months of my career ending it sourly.

My job and money had become my idols of self-worth and security. An idol is something that we love, want, desire, treasure, or enjoy more than God. Relying on an idol can divert our attention away from our problem or give us confidence our idol is all we need to solve our problem. Examples of idols that do this are things we enjoy but cause harm such as overeating, smoking, alcohol, drugs, or an activity (my job), a person who we count on, or money. The problem is still there, and the idol won't solve it. When instead we humble ourselves and turn to God, we face our problems. God helps us in ways that nothing or nobody else can. After I retired, I learned that what is most important is what is on our inside rather than our outside, God has a better purpose for me and gives my life more meaning than my job did, I love God above anything else, only God can deliver me from struggles life poses, one always wants more money even if they have what they need, and God gives me much more than what money can buy.

 We turn away from idols and to the all-powerful God who can deliver us from our trials.

15. THE RAINSTORM
Run to God

The name of the LORD is a strong tower;
The righteous run to it and are safe.
PROVERBS 18:10

On a day with few clouds, my husband and I left our house for a long walk. Rain didn't seem like a threat. A couple of hours later, dark clouds came, and it started raining. It didn't take long for it to turn to a downpour. We weren't prepared. Rain would have quickly soaked through our clothing, given us wet hair, and caused us to be cold. We saw a carport. With no hesitation, we ran to it. Being under the carport was relaxing and peaceful. During the 20 minutes we stood there, we were concerned the owners might ask us to leave. But no one objected to our being there. How fortunate as the carport kept us perfectly dry and safe from the rain. On our way home after the rain stopped, we were so relieved we had found such a wonderful place to wait.

Like the rainstorm, trials can come with no warning. We can't prepare for them. While the carport gave physical safety, during our trials God gives believers spiritual safety when we run to Him in prayer. Our desire to run to Him comes easily when we understand who God is and what He can do. The name of the LORD stands for God Himself. It encompasses His character. He is perfect in all His ways, makes no mistakes, and is all-powerful. We would be fools to not rely on God! Yet, we sometimes rely on idols such as money or people instead of God. When we put them aside, in trust, we can run to our loving and welcoming Father with confidence. In return, God will:

- Comfort us by supplying emotional strength when we are weak.
- Empower us by lifting us when we fall from the trial overwhelming us.
- Sustain us by replacing anxiety with peace and giving us hope in times of despair.
- Lead us on the right path when we obey His word and pray.
- Offer a way of escape when tempted.

What God gives is always sufficient. It is perfect and goes beyond what we humans can do for ourselves or each other. While many of us can't physically run, all believers can run to His safety in prayer. He is always there.

 There are ways that only God can help amid trials.

16. LOST IN CANADA
Why We Should Ask God for Direction

Trust in the LORD with all your heart,
And lean not on your own understanding;
In all your ways acknowledge Him,
And He shall direct your paths.
PROVERBS 3:5-6

On a vacation in Canada, a car ferry dropped my husband, Ed, and me off. Road signs were wooden slats with a town and an arrow painted on them pointing the way. They gave no mileage and had vague descriptions. Our map didn't make sense. After much driving, we returned three times to our starting point to try again. Each time, we passed by a gas station, but Ed didn't want to ask for directions. Why should he? Wherever we ventured, we had always been able to navigate to our destination. Out of options, we succumbed and asked. With their directions, we drove directly to our destination.

Just as Ed didn't want to ask for directions, we may not ask God when we need direction in life. Below are reasons why we do that followed by the fallacy of this way of thinking in parentheses.

- *HABIT.* We get used to making decisions (but that doesn't mean we make the right decisions).
- *PRIDE.* We would be admitting failure (failure will happen when we take the wrong path).
- *TIME.* It takes too long to ask (yet we can waste much time on the wrong path).

- *TRIVIAL.* It is too trivial to bother asking (nothing is too trivial for God).
- *SELF CONFIDENCE.* We can figure it out on our own (or not).
- *EMBARRASSED.* We don't want to show our ignorance (yet being on the wrong path is embarrassing).

When we lean on our own understanding, we may think we know which direction we should go in life. Instead, we can end up lost in much more serious ways than Ed and I did. We have the best guide, God, the creator of the universe who loves us, wants to help, and is always available. We are the problem when we don't humble ourselves and take time to ask Him. The more times we ask in prayer and follow through, the easier it is to do and more natural it becomes. God may lead us on a path we wouldn't have even known about or considered.

 The best guidance we can get comes from God who is always available.

17. THE WATER JUGS
Cast our Cares on God

Casting all your care upon Him, for He cares for you.
1 PETER 5:7

My dad was a scoutmaster for the Boy Scouts when I was a child. To prepare the scouts for a hike lasting several days, he took them on day hikes. On one hike, he wanted them to become accustomed to carrying packs but didn't want them to carry much weight at first. To do that, they used large empty water jugs to fill the space their gear would take up. After several miles, one of the scouts, Bob, was much more exhausted than the other scouts. This puzzled my dad as Bob was in great shape and had done so well on other hikes. Bob shared with my dad how heavy the pack was and how much more difficult that made the hike. It turned out Bob had filled the jugs with water. When Bob found out his error, he was relieved. The rest of the hike went much easier.

No one would put unnecessary weight in their backpack. Yet we sometimes carry around our anxieties when it isn't necessary. This wears us out and affects our ability to deal with life. God, our loving Father, is there to help when we pray and cast our cares on Him. God can choose to change our circumstance. All powerful and in control, God can stop big trials, like directing hurricanes away from land or curing cancer. He can also stop trials no matter how small in each of our lives that cause us anxiety. When He ends our trial, our anxiety disappears. We feel the load lighten much like the scout who got rid of his excess weight. What a relief! Alternatively, God can choose to not change our circumstance. However, He doesn't leave us to cope with it alone or in our own strength. God addresses our emotions that cause anxiety by giving us help such as wisdom, peace, calm, and confidence. No matter how or when God chooses to relieve our anxieties, He lightens the load we carry.

 Our hike through life is so much easier when God lightens our load.

18. THE WATER BOTTLE
Nothing Is Too Hard for God

*"Behold, I am the LORD, the God of all flesh.
Is there anything too hard for Me?"*
JEREMIAH 32:27

A coworker, Ed, laughed when he tried to walk faster than me. Few could keep up with him and he was impressed when I did. The sparkle in his eye led to marriage. Two of our favorite activities were walking and hiking. The beginning stages of my ALS was the end of me being able to keep up with Ed, but that didn't stop us from being as active as possible. On hikes, Ed sometimes went ahead a bit. Eventually, I would find him waiting for me. On one occasion, that didn't happen. Instead, I found his water bottle in the middle of the trail. I knew what it meant. Ed couldn't cope with the slow pace my disease dictated. Lacking patience, he wanted to walk at a faster pace that we had once enjoyed together. Not able to face me to explain, he left the water bottle. Ed meant no harm, reasoned I would figure out he went ahead, and knew I would be okay on the well-marked trail. However, I was disappointed and sad. About 40 minutes later, I made it out of the forested area and saw him a couple of miles ahead.

Ed was a loving husband who did what he could to support me, but like all of us, had his limitations. To cope, Ed chose to temporarily escape by leaving me behind on the trail. If we had had God in our lives at that time, I believe he would have responded differently.

When we exceed our limitations, whether we are the one in the trial or the loved one supporting someone in a trial, God can help us in ways we can't help ourselves. Unlike us with all our limitations, nothing is too hard for God who will never be deterred from helping us in a trial. In answer to our prayers, God can:

- Fill us with peace, joy, and calmness that can only come from Him.
- Help us to forgive and be kind to those who wrong us.
- Instill patience when it isn't natural.
- Give us confidence to face a situation or the future when we acknowledge He is in control.
- Show us the right direction to take.

When I have struggled, God gave me all these gifts in answer to my prayers. They were miracles as I couldn't have had them on my own.

 God's wondrous help is only a prayer away.

SECTION 3
RELATIONSHIPS
WITH PEOPLE

19. THE NECKTIES
Fellowship

But if we walk in the light as He is in the light, we have fellowship with one another, and the blood of Jesus Christ His Son cleanses us from all sin.
1 JOHN 1:7

My engineering office manager, Al, had a knack for encouraging fellowship. As a result, we put our differences aside to help each other with our shared interest of finishing assignments efficiently and correctly for critical projects. In addition to rallying us together, Al was well known for persuading supervisors to wear neckties. So, on the day Al retired, all thirty people who worked for him wore neckties, even the women. Al got a big laugh when he saw us in neckties throughout the day, especially those he least expected to wear one. We made history with a photograph in the shipyard newspaper.

The fellowship in the office was based on a shared interest and the leadership of a unique man. Christian fellowship is based on shared beliefs, convictions, and values and the leadership of our Lord, Jesus Christ. This fellowship is unique with many principles, outcomes, and rewards that are superior to anything in the world.

- All believers are considered equal despite many personal differences.
- Christian fellowship is the largest fellowship reaching every believer worldwide.
- Talking about God excites us.

- We help keep each other on the right path when we have tough decisions to make or the physical world tugs us in the wrong direction.
- We enjoy sharing or expressing our prayer needs, praying for each other, and sharing about answered prayers.
- We learn from God's word and from each other about agape love that is not sentimental but sacrificial.
- We lovingly encourage, instruct, and correct one another.
- We willingly humble ourselves and admit our faults, weaknesses, and failures knowing we will be received with love.
- We share our joy, comfort, hope, and peace in God.

With God's help and guidance, this fellowship helps us grow spiritually and progress in our walk with God. It ties us together in the family of God with our brothers and sisters in Christ.

 The most important and fulfilling human fellowship available to us is with other believers.

20. THANKSGIVING TURKEY
Sharpening Each Other's Wits

As iron sharpens iron, So a man sharpens the countenance of his friend.
PROVERBS 27:17

When I was growing up, we had many family gatherings with 20 to 30 people. On Thanksgiving, we always had turkey. Back then, it was a highlight as we only had turkey once a year. The turkey came out of the oven golden brown and looked scrumptious. While others put everything on the table, one person carved the turkey. The children watched in anticipation ready to grab a hot, fresh piece. I liked it when it was my dad's turn to do the carving. Before carving, my dad ran the knife blade along a rod several times to sharpen it. He made a production out of it for the children. When my dad figured the knife was sharp enough, he started carving the turkey. Yum!

The more my dad sharpened the knife, the better it worked. Sharpening was done in biblical times by rubbing iron against iron. This concept of sharpening to improve performance also pertains to sharpening each other's wits by engaging in intelligent discussions on a variety of subjects. We benefit from these discussions by learning, gaining perspectives, refining our thoughts, taking better actions, and solving problems in ways that we couldn't have done on our own. It is gratifying when people's faces light up with understanding as we share. If we don't sharpen each other's wits, it would be like not sharpening the knife. Just as the knife wouldn't work as well, we wouldn't do as well. However, we must be careful when we are discussing moral principles. We live in an evil world ruled by Satan and encouraged by much of the media. Societal influences can make evil paths seem morally acceptable. But what many consider acceptable is unbiblical and can do a lot of harm. We can have the most confidence in sharpening wits with mature believers. Others may not live by biblical moral principles. So, it is important to ensure that if we follow what they say, it is biblical. If uncertain, consult trusted mature believers. It pleases them to ensure we are on God's path. Additionally, before acting we pray to God to make certain we are in His will.

 Sharpening one another's wits with God's moral principles benefits everyone involved.

21. THE FLAT TIRE
Seeking Wise Counsel

The way of a fool is right in his own eyes,
But he who heeds counsel is wise.
PROVERBS 12:15

A friend, Garth, came by as my husband, Ed, and I were packing our truck for a camping trip. Garth seemed concerned about the tires on our truck and used a coin to measure their tread. He warned us we needed to replace our tires and that we should do it before the trip. Garth claimed he had lots of experience with tires. Though Ed was no expert on tires, he knew a lot about vehicles, did all his own maintenance, and was certain the tires wouldn't be a problem. I could have said something, but I didn't. Neither of us wanted to delay our trip, so we left the next day as planned. In the late afternoon, we got a flat tire. We put the spare on, but it didn't have enough air in it to safely drive a long distance. Gratefully, we made it to a gas station just before it was scheduled to close. Had they not been open, we might not have made it safely to the next station. The next day, our priority was to go to a tire shop to get all the tires replaced. We were fortunate as our situation could have ended much worse.

Obviously, Ed and I should have taken Garth's advice. Sometimes, when we think we know what is best for us or people suggest something we don't want to do, we do as we please. Other times, our confidence can prevent us from seeking advice on a subject, even when we don't know much about it. We can get obstinate or defensive when corrected. These traits can cause us to act like fools as Ed and I did. Instead, we are much better off when we seek wise counsel. Teaching and wisdom from our all-knowing God that we find in the Bible tells us how to live righteously, guides us, and helps us. We supplement this with prayer and reliance on the Holy Spirit. Mature Christians can help us with our spiritual and ethical questions. For practical issues, we rely on people with experience. I have used all of these to relieve depression, anxiety, and fear, get guidance, help me deal with people, and gain knowledge.

 We make the most of our lives by looking upward to God and outward to the right people rather than inward to ourselves.

22. SUPPORTING SHEREE TO GO TO CHURCH
How to Treat Others

*"And just as you want men to do to you,
you also do to them likewise."*
LUKE 6:31

Sheree suffered from muscular dystrophy. Because of it, she wasn't comfortable going to church. A church elder asked me to talk to her. Because of my shyness, reaching out to her was outside my comfort zone. However, because I had experienced similar struggles, without hesitation I said yes. Sheree had physical concerns to figure out and emotional issues to address about what people would think. After several weeks of talking on the phone, we became friends and made plans for her to go to church. What a wonderful day it was when she arrived at church with her face lit up and a big smile. People flocked to her and wanted to get to know her. Afterwards, Sheree was so happy when she shared with me about going to church and looked forward to returning. Her outings came just in time. After attending church three times, she became ill and died. While in the hospital for her last week here on earth, what fond memories she had of her church outings where she blessed many, including me.

When I struggled the way Sheree did, I would have appreciated someone to help me as I helped her. The Bible tells us to treat others as we would want to be treated in the same circumstance. These opportunities don't always come to us, and we may need to look for them. That happened when I shared what to expect with many people making decisions about getting a trach or feeding tube. In return, it brought joy to my heart. To exercise this Christlike love, we don't need a deep understanding of peoples' circumstances, we just need to respond appropriately to the best of our ability. When we struggle, we can pray for help. God will give us the perfect answer.

 How we treat others reflects our walk with God.

23. UNABLE TO OPEN THE DOOR
Sharing One Another's Burdens

Bear one another's burdens,
and so fulfill the law of Christ.
GALATIANS 6:2

In my working years, I had to use one cane, and then two as my disease progressed. Even with such difficulty walking, I didn't need any special accommodations at my job. That changed when my office moved to another building. To my surprise, despite great determination using all my might, I couldn't open the door to my office. People who arrived when I did opened the door, but at the end of the day, I had to ask a coworker to open the door. In the middle of the day, I sometimes had to go to another building for business. That was the worst because a coworker had to open the door when I left and when I returned. Negative thoughts occupied my mind during the long walk between the door and my office. "This is so humiliating…no one else has this issue…I hate my disease." My coworkers had a different response. They were always willing to stop what they were doing to help. They comforted me when I expressed my feelings.

Because I couldn't accept my limitations, I was reluctant to let people help me, even though they were willing. As an unbeliever who didn't rely on God at the time, this sinful pride resulted in me carrying a heavy burden. Our burdens exist because we live in an evil and fallen world where we can struggle physically, emotionally, or morally with trials, temptation, or sin. As believers, we can have victory over our struggles by relying on God. However, when we still have a tough time, keeping burdens to ourselves can increase our struggles and cause suffering. Instead, when we help with one another's burdens, they become lighter or disappear. Reaching out for help may be difficult because of pride, embarrassment, or awkwardness. We can pray for God's help to overcome these obstacles. When others ask us for help, we carefully listen before speaking, don't judge, and respond with love, sensitivity, and compassion. We do this by the power of the Holy Spirit with Christlike love. If a problem stumps us, we admit it and pray to God for guidance. Next, we may need to ask a mature Christian for advice. Sometimes we just need someone to listen.

 Sharing burdens blesses all involved.

24. BUMP HER CARS
God Gives Better Ways Than Retaliating

Do not repay anyone evil for evil. Be careful to do what is right in the eyes of everyone.
ROMANS 12:17

On a family vacation at Disneyland, my brother and I, ages 13 and 8, enjoyed one of the rides where we drove cars on a child-friendly track. A metal strip in the middle of the road prevented us from veering off the track. The third time we went on the ride, I got stuck behind stopped cars. Bash! My brother rear-ended me at full speed. I turned around to see him laughing. It wasn't funny to me. These weren't bumper cars. However, knowing people wouldn't resist, the designers constructed the bumpers to take the impact. Even so, rear-ending another car could still cause injuries and there were signs saying it was not allowed. All that aside, no way would I let my brother get away with what he did. Next time, I made certain he was in front of me. I rear-ended him. Success!

We were children doing what children do. Still, we can apply this scenario to adults when someone does something we don't like or when we are wronged. Our temptation can be to take immediate retaliation. However, it is wrong for us to be the accuser, judge, and decide on the sentence. Actions we take can be in the heat of passion and lead to an unwarranted and inappropriate response. What if I had physically hurt my brother when I rear-ended him? Vengeance is up to God when called for. Instead of retaliation, God gives us better options. We ask God to reveal His plan to us. To carry out the plan, we pray for calmness, kindness, and gentleness. When we address the situation, we forgive and accept suffering for what they did. The proper approach in my example would have been to calmly, kindly, and gently share with my brother why I didn't like getting rear-ended, ask him to not do it, forgive him, and accept that he rear-ended me. God may also guide us to walk away from a situation and just pray for the offender.

 Meet hostility with God's perfect guidance.

25. SUNSETS
Address Anger before Bedtime

"Be angry, and do not sin": do not let the sun go down on your wrath, nor give place to the devil.
EPHESIANS 4:26-27

Campgrounds on the Oregon coast offered my husband and me beautiful sunsets. At the end of the day, we walked the short distance from our campsite to the beach to position ourselves for a splendid view of it. The sunset mesmerized us, especially when there were clouds that reflected yellow, orange, red, and purple. After the sun disappeared from the horizon, it got dark very quickly. That meant change from the many activities of the day to settling into the tranquility of evening that preceded going to bed. At home, though we didn't pay attention to sunsets, we did experience that there was a time to put the day's events and worries behind us so we could sleep soundly.

The sun setting symbolizes our tranquil time prior to bedtime. Before we go to bed, we are to address issues that led to anger that day. This is anything that caused damage from what someone did or said. Anger is righteous when we are defending God's word. Anger is sinful when it is in response to a personal wrong. If we don't address it and move forward as though it didn't happen, it opens the door for Satan to enter. New emotions of hurt, bitterness, hatred, or revenge can arise and fester. I have experienced sleepless nights because of this. Also, issues will be harder to resolve later. God gives us better ways. We are to apologize and ask for forgiveness from both God and those involved. When we don't know what to say, we can pray to God for guidance. The Holy Spirit will help us with courage and the right words. If others don't or won't apologize to us, we can pray for God's help to forgive them. When I took these approaches, I experienced blessings with mended and strengthened relationships.

 Addressing anger God's way before we go to bed leads to sound sleep.

26. DOING OUR BEST
Working Heartily Shows Our Faith

And whatever you do, do it heartily,
as to the Lord and not to men.
COLOSSIANS 3:23

When my husband and I transferred from a naval
shipyard in California to Washington, one of my duties
was the engineering to convert the Cleanroom for more
stringent cleanliness requirements. The Cleanroom was
where the most precise cleaning for naval systems took
place. To do that, we designed the room with special
materials and filtration, it needed daily cleaning, and
workers measured its cleanliness. Anyone entering the
room dressed in special gloves, booties, coveralls, and a
head covering. On a visit to the Cleanroom under
renovation, I saw a worker cleaning residue on the floor
from relocated equipment. I had no idea who he was. He
was lying on his belly using a tiny brush and scraper. It
looked so odd. There were easier ways to clean the
residue without lying on his belly, but this was how he
chose to do it. What a lowly and tedious job. I figured he
must have been a newer worker to get this assignment.
As I watched, I could tell that removing every bit of
residue was important to him and that he put his heart
into whatever assigned to do. In years to come, we
would work together a lot. As a senior worker in his
office, he was an asset to the shipyard whom I would
come to respect.

This worker could have had the mundane task assigned to someone else. Instead, he did it in a way that was effective without a care as to what he looked like. Just as he did, we are to do our best at all we do. Our mindset should be that we are serving or working for God, not people, like a servant who loves his master. We are an example to others of a Christian willing to do all types of work with nothing beneath us. Fittingly, this worker's last name was "Best" and that is what we should give in all we do.

 Doing our best shows our faithfulness.

27. THE ENGINE PARTS
We All Serve a Purpose in the Body of Christ

As each one has received a gift, minister it to one
another, as good stewards of the manifold grace of God.
1 PETER 4:10

When our car needed its engine repaired, my husband and I took on the challenge. After we removed parts from the engine, we removed the engine with a hoist and took the engine to a friend to repair. As we put the parts back on, the variety and their functions amazed me. Individually, they did nothing. When put together correctly and with all parts functioning properly, the car would start and work. Every detail mattered such as a hose or spark plug gap. After assembling the parts, with great anticipation my husband turned the key. We both smiled and said with excitement, "It works!" It didn't just start, it worked fantastic for many years.

Just as the car needed all the parts working together, so does the body of Christ with every believer having a purpose using their skills or God-given gift(s). We develop skills throughout our lives, and we receive a gift or gifts at the time of our salvation. These talents and gifts serve the body of Christ, not just when we meet in the building we call a church, but all the time. Using a God-given gift feels spectacular as we experience God's power that is beyond what we have on our own. However, even if we aren't gifted in an area, God has given us all some ability to play a part. For instance, if a believer has the gift of faith, they have more confidence in God's abilities than most, though all believers have some faith. One who has the gift to evangelize may do it more naturally than most, but all believers can and should proclaim the gospel. Those who God has gifted can encourage and help others who struggle in that area. While some jobs may not seem as important as others, they are all necessary, just as a car won't work without a hose. Being jealous of someone with a gift that we want is inappropriate as God chooses the gifts. This isn't about us, but the body of Christ. In whatever way we serve, it is an honor and we do it with zeal. It brings joy. When we each contribute, the body of Christ functions at its best.

 When we use our skills or gift(s), we are bodybuilders.

28. THE BIRTHDAY PARTIES
Looking out for Each Other's Interests

Let each of you look out not only for his own interests,
but also for the interests of others.
PHILIPPIANS 2:4

At my office, we had huge potluck parties for major
holidays. After many years of this, I noticed people
having birthday parties. They started small and rare with
a few close friends, and then grew bigger for the more
popular employees and became more common.
However, though unintended, this left out some people. I
wondered if our boss would notice and put a stop to it.
Eventually, a couple of people involved in the parties
finally noticed those left out. They approached our boss
and came back with a plan. Rather than celebrating
individual birthdays, every month we would have a large
cake everyone could eat to celebrate that month's
birthdays. I remember cakes, names of people called out
who had a birthday that month, and satisfaction in a
great solution.

The plan they came up with looked out for their own
interests by continuing to have celebrations, but also for
interests of others by recognizing everyone. To look out
for each other's interests, we need to:

- *PRAY*. Pray for God's help and guidance and for
  one another.
- *OBSERVE*. We may be blind to opportunities unless
  we take our eyes off ourselves and look at others.
- *BE HUMBLE*. This gives us the right attitude.

- *BE KIND*. Consider others' personality and the trials they are facing.
- *SACRIFICE*. Put the priorities of others ahead of our desires.
- *STRATEGIZE*. Implement a plan considering the interests of all involved.

When we succeed, everyone involved will reap thankfulness and joy. This doesn't just apply to the temporal, but also the spiritual when we reach out to unbelievers to share the gospel. This not only looks out for their interests when God opens their eyes and saves their soul, but also ours in potentially gaining a new brother or sister in Christ.

Looking out for the interests of others profits all and pleases God.

29. OVERCOMING MY SHYNESS
Qualities We Need to Share Our Faith

But sanctify the Lord God in your hearts,
and always be ready to give a defense
to everyone who asks you a reason for the hope
that is in you, with meekness and fear.
1 PETER 3:15

All my life I was shy. Like so many, I feared public speaking. At work, though I was quite familiar with the subject matter, I was quiet at meetings and gave minimal input. One day, I attended a meeting with about thirty people to discuss execution of several jobs. Attendees included an intimidating mix of workers and managers from my office and various trades. When one of the jobs I was working on came up, they didn't understand the technical issues and headed in the wrong direction. I couldn't let that happen. Without hesitation, I stood up, calmly and confidently explained the issues, and answered their questions. Everyone in the room was surprised, including me. The discussion changed to the right track. That day, I took a big step to overcoming my shyness. In future meetings, my input was requested, delivered, and valued.

Shyness is a struggle for many. There may be times we are shy about sharing our faith with others. I overcame my shyness because I had a desire to share, knowledge that gave me confidence, and experience from my job. These gave me confidence so I could deliver calmly. All of these apply to sharing our faith as described below. Additionally, we have our Helper, the Holy Spirit.

- *DESIRE.* With our passion for God, we want to share.
- *KNOWLEDGE.* Bible knowledge gives us confidence.
- *EXPERIENCE.* With a living God working in our life, we can share our experiences about how God has changed us, helped us, and given us hope. This adds credibility as it goes beyond head knowledge. Our wonderful God deserves our praise.
- *DELIVERY.* It isn't just about what we say, but how we deliver it. We uphold a humble demeanor and don't brag. Our tone of voice is steady and welcoming. If people raise their voices, we keep ours calm and respond with our treasury of knowledge and experience.
- *HELPER.* The Holy Spirit gives us guidance and wisdom.

 Sharing about our faith feels fantastic, blesses us and others, and is our most vital interaction.

30. THE LOST TOURISTS
Overcoming Struggles to Evangelize

Preach the word! Be ready in season and out of season.
2 TIMOTHY 4:2A

I often went on bicycle rides after work and on weekends. It was relaxing on the quiet tree-lined roads with few cars. After nine miles of non-stop riding, there was a stop sign and a turnout for cars. On one of my rides, I was surprised to see a car there with the driver waving for me to stop. Several reasons I shouldn't stop occurred to me. They might pose a danger. My muscles that I warmed in the hills would get cold when I was about to face a steep mountain climb. It would mess up the time I kept track of for every ride. Certainly, they would understand if I gave a friendly wave and apologetically told them I couldn't stop. I stopped. They looked like they were in need, and that was more important than my reasons not to stop. I learned they were lost tourists who needed directions. After this happened a few times, I started carrying a map in the small bag under my bicycle seat. Lost tourists were surprised I carried a map to help them and relieved when I showed them where they had made a wrong turn.

Though I had plenty of reasons to ride by, I stopped to help the lost tourists. Similarly, we should choose to take opportunities to proclaim the gospel to the spiritually lost. However, sometimes we don't because of struggles or misconceptions. Examples are below along with how we can overcome them.

- We don't know what to say. Overcome. Practice and know that the Holy Spirit will lead.
- It is an inconvenient time. Overcome. When God gives us an opportunity, take it!
- We fear people will refute the message with hostility. Overcome. Pray. Some may respond that way, but what if they don't and we miss an opportunity?
- We are not good at it. Overcome. Pray for courage and guidance. God does the work of changing their heart.

God calls on us Christians to proclaim the gospel to unbelievers at every opportunity. This means when conditions are ideal or not, i.e., in or out of season. I have heard many accounts of people saved by God after Christians evangelized in challenging circumstances.

 The most important task we do is to proclaim the gospel.

31. SHARING MY PASSION ABOUT SOLAR ENERGY
Proclaiming the Gospel Despite Opposition

*For the message of the cross is foolishness
to those who are perishing, but to us who are
being saved it is the power of God.*
1 CORINTHIANS 1:18

Solar power interested me when I attended University. Back then in the 1980s, while many rejected it, I understood its applications and benefits. I figured it would eventually gain popularity. That did happen, but it took twenty years. My first experience sharing about it was in a speech class. Some were receptive. Others disagreed and thought I was foolish, though they listened. A few were surprised at the information I gave and became convinced solar power was practical for homes and profitable. A year later, I took an engineering class in solar power. The following semester in a laboratory class, two of my classmates and I chose to do an experiment with a solar collector. For our senior design project, the three of us were the only ones who designed a solar power system. Again, responses from my classmates were varied.

We don't hesitate to proclaim what we are passionate about even if it isn't popular. Similarly, we Christians should proclaim the gospel with the same doggedness and enthusiasm. However, sometimes we can find it difficult to do so. Why is that? For most subjects, people willingly listen to what we have to say. While they may disagree, we can continue with friendly discussions. However, for the gospel people may not be receptive. Discussion isn't welcome. This can be distressing because what we know with certainty as the power of God, they consider foolish. It hurts more than disagreeing on other subjects because it is their soul at stake. We shouldn't let this discourage us. God needs to open their heart. For those whose hearts God has opened, God uses us, broken people, to proclaim the gospel to bring Him glory. He is by our side as the Holy Spirit helps us with what to say. Though rejection can be difficult, when we approach humbly, we won't harm our relationship. It is the least we can do considering Jesus' blood saved our soul.

 What an honor that God chooses us to proclaim the gospel and what a blessing to experience God saving souls.

32. GIVING TO CHARITY
What Are Good Works?

*But someone will say, "You have faith, and I have
works." Show me your faith without your works,
and I will show you my faith by my works.*
JAMES 2:18

At my job, I had an annual opportunity to give to
charities through the Combined Federal Campaign. I
chose the charities from an extensive list. My donations
were anonymous, so the charities couldn't send inquiries
to my house asking for more money or share my
information with other charities. What I gave was
deducted from each paycheck. There was no excuse to
not give. Each office had a goal for the total their
employees would give. Managers had bragging rights if
their office met their goal and were looked down on if
they didn't. Coworkers volunteered to encourage us to
give. People who didn't give were badgered. I gave just
to prevent that.

If I had been a Christian, I believe that my response to
charitable giving would have been different. Perhaps I
would have outwardly thanked God that I could afford to
give, asked for His guidance in choosing a charity, and
prayed for that charity's success. Then my giving would
have been a good work rather than the way I gave as an
obligation. What are good works? They are acts we do to
glorify God. Good works can be small mundane acts we
do throughout our day or large acts we plan. We carry
them out in obedience to God showing our love toward

Him. Good works show our faith that would otherwise be invisible to people. Our good works must come after salvation for two reasons. Good works don't earn our salvation because it is a gift from God (Eph. 2:8-9). Also, millions of good works wouldn't make up for even one sin. Only the blood of Jesus can do that. Secondly, unbelievers can do works that are good, or even great, not prideful, and out of love for others, but they can't do them out of love for God. Only believers love God.

 Good works make our faith visible to others.

33. GLASSBLOWING
We Are God's Workmanship Created
for Good Works

For we are His workmanship,
created in Christ Jesus for good works,
which God prepared beforehand
that we should walk in them.
EPHESIANS 2:10

On a vacation, my husband and I visited a glassblowing shop. The process captivated us. The artist rolled his blowpipe on molten glass in a furnace to collect some. He added color and design by dipping into crushed colored glass. Much careful effort in rotating and blowing on the pipe resulted in the piece reaching the intended size. Throughout the process, small tools came into play to create shape and patterns. The artist continually worked on his piece. The breathtaking pieces available to buy were of varying sizes, shapes, colors, and purposes. We bought a few pieces for ourselves and as gifts.

With a vision in mind of what he would make, the glassblower took a molten gob of glass and made pieces of useful art. Similarly, God has a plan for believers' good works. We are His workmanship. God changes us from an unbeliever without purpose into a beautiful and useful masterpiece for His good works. The process started for us when we became a new creation at our salvation. God turned our heart from stone to flesh so that He could shape us for His purpose. God endowed us with skills and gave us spiritual gifts that enable us to do the good works He chose for us. Throughout our life, God allows us to go through trials and experiences that shape us and influence what we become, ever more like Christ. This affects our good works. God's power is superior to the human effort of the glassblower and always produces the result He desires. We want to do good works that glorify God to please Him. Doing them gratifies us. Good works are fruit from our salvation, not the cause of it. That doesn't mean they automatically happen. We find God's plan for us by studying God's word, praying, and watching for opportunities. Next, we do what He tells us. Good works can vary in size from small to large such as encouraging someone or pouring our time and energy into a ministry.

Good works are the most enjoyable and meaningful work we do.

SECTION 4
INSIGHTS ON SIN

34. THE FREEDOM PARADOX
Earthly Versus Godly Freedom

But God be thanked that though you were slaves of sin,
yet you obeyed from the heart that form of doctrine to
which you were delivered. And having been set free from
sin, you became slaves of righteousness.
ROMANS 6:17-18

After I graduated from high school, I moved away to
attend University. When the airplane touched the ground
and I arrived at my apartment, life changed. No longer
under my parent's rules, I was finally free! No one was
watching over me. I could do whatever and whenever I
wanted. I would make my own rules and decisions that
weren't as stringent. If I did something wrong, I
wouldn't need to confess it. Freedom was wonderful!

   At the time, it felt great to do as I pleased. This desire
is our human nature. As unbelievers, we perceived it as
freedom. While we preferred living this way, we weren't
free as sin enslaved us. This is the freedom paradox. We
didn't even recognize it as a problem living in the
darkness of evil. Our outlook changed when God shined
on our heart and Satan no longer blinded us to the light.
We became believers in what Jesus did in His death,
burial, and resurrection. As believers, we are changed,
favoring to live in the light of God. Our relationship with
God is opposite of what we had considered as freedom,
yet we are free in much different and better ways. Below
are contrasts to freedom we believers experience and
enjoy.

- We welcome God to watch over us as His care is superior to what we can do on our own.
- We welcome His control rather than our feeble ways that fall quite short of His.
- We welcome God's rules of righteousness that are more stringent than we ever had, but always correct, giving us a better life in many ways.
- We want to obey God and be in His will rather than do as we please because He knows best, it pleases God, His path is wonderful, and it delights us.
- When we sin, we admit it by repenting to God who always forgives rather than keeping it to ourselves.
- We will have eternal freedom when we enjoy bliss in heaven with God rather than suffering.

 Freedom is walking with God rather than rebelling against Him.

35. THE MIRROR
Being a Doer of God's Word

For if anyone is a hearer of the word and not a doer,
he is like a man observing his natural face in a mirror;
for he observes himself, goes away, and immediately
forgets what kind of man he was.
JAMES 1:23-24

As a teenager, I watched my friend apply makeup in front of a bathroom mirror. She needed the well-lit mirror to see details. It was quite a process that took a long time. After cleansing her face, she applied makeup on her entire face followed by special attention around her eyes. Lastly came her lips. Getting it right was important to her. This wasn't something that interested me; I spent little time in front of a mirror getting ready for my day. I was satisfied with that. Years later when I married, my husband jokingly called me low maintenance. We both considered that a good quality.

A mirror shows our outside. When we hear God's word, it is like a mirror that reveals to us what is on our inside, our spiritual life. If we walk away after only a brief look, we will not learn specifics about our spiritual needs. What little we learn we will quickly forget, so we will not be able to act on it. When that happens, we are a hearer of the word. Instead, to be a doer of the word, just as my friend took a detailed look in the mirror, we need to study God's word to understand how it applies to our lives. We may not like what we hear when God's word contradicts what we had thought to be correct, forbids what we want to do, or convicts us of sin we don't want to admit. However, we should welcome what God's word teaches us so that we know what we need to change to obey God. Being a doer isn't always easy. We may need help to act on what we hear by praying and reaching out to mature Christians for advice. It is crucial because being a doer progresses our walk with God and repenting returns us to God's fellowship. Pleasing God by "grooming our inside" is much more important than worrying about what people notice when we groom our outside.

 Being a doer of the word keeps us on the right path.

36. VALENTINE'S DAY
Ways God Loves

The LORD is compassionate and gracious,
slow to anger, abounding in love.
PSALM 103:8

On Valentine's Day, my husband, Ed, and I agreed to not do anything special or exchange gifts, though we loved each other dearly. One year, Ed couldn't resist his idea. As I got dressed for work, I found love notes on small pieces of paper tactfully placed in my shoes, socks, pants, and blouse. Ed normally didn't watch me dress, but that morning, he took pleasure in my reactions. With each note, we shared the gratitude for the romantic and caring love we had for each other.

We show several types of love for people by our actions. God promises us the greatest love of all, agape, that goes well beyond what people can do as He loves us in these ways.

- *UNCONDITIONALLY.* We don't earn or deserve God's love as it is by His grace (Eph. 2:4-5). Our love is conditional.
- *INFINITELY.* God loves us more than we can ever love Him (Psalm 108:4). Our love has limits.
- *SACRIFICIALLY.* We are all sinners deserving of death, yet Jesus gave his life to pay for our sins so that we could enjoy eternal life in heaven (Rom. 3:23-24). People would rarely give their life for a loved one, let alone someone unworthy.

- *PERMANENTLY.* Nothing can separate us from God's love (Rom. 8:38-39). People leave loved ones over disputes.
- *FATHERLY.* We are God's children, and He wants the best for us (1 John 3:1). No one cares for us as much as God and He is always there.
- *GRACIOUSLY.* God always forgives sin when we confess and repent from our hearts (1 John 1:9). People can struggle with forgiveness.

We can't love as completely as God. When we understand and realize how much God loves us, it gives us a deep sense of relief, comfort, joy, and hope. In return, we show our love for God by obeying Him. Common sense tells us it should be easy to obey as God's perfect ways are superior to our flawed ones. Yet, with our sin nature, we don't always obey. So, when sin lures us, we give our best effort in turning away from it and to our loving God. When we struggle, we pray, and God enables us to be victorious.

In return for God's great love, it is a joy to give Him our devotion and obedience.

37. TUG OF WAR
The Battle between Our Flesh and the Holy Spirit

For the flesh lusts against the Spirit, and the Spirit against the flesh; and these are contrary to one another, so that you do not do the things that you wish. But if you are led by the Spirit, you are not under the law.
GALATIANS 5:17-18

In the game of tug of war, competitors tug in opposite directions on a rope until one side passes through an agreed upon point such as a mark on the rope or, for the casual game, a mud puddle. Success isn't just a matter of strength, but technique, wit, cooperation, and heeding orders for when to pull and rest. As Christians, we find ourselves in a tug of war between our sinful flesh and the Holy Spirit that influences us in opposite directions. It should be an easy battle with the Holy Spirit winning, but it doesn't always work that way. Also, rather than lasting for minutes as a typical tug of war game, it can last hours, days, or even longer.

Why are we in this spiritual tug of war? Because when we became Christians God chose to not immediately take away our old sinful nature. Because of this our old nature becomes evident as we slowly change through sanctification, the progressive work of God to make us more like Jesus. This happens as we turn away from sin and obey God. Sanctification doesn't happen easily. With both our sinful flesh and the Holy Spirit at work, we experience conflict between what we want to do and how we know we should live. These draw us in opposite directions. This tug of war will exist until we are in heaven where we will no longer have our sinful nature. Until then, we can stop the tug of war by yielding to the Holy Spirit whenever we have conflict. Afterwards, it feels right in our soul. We won that tug of war with our sin, though there will be new ones. The more tug of war matches we have, the easier it becomes to win, and our matches will be shorter and reduce in number.

 We are winners at spiritual tug of war and in life when we yield to the Holy Spirit.

38. THE MUD PUDDLE
How to Repent Properly

The sacrifices of God are a broken spirit,
A broken and a contrite heart—
These, O God, You will not despise.
PSALM 51:17

My husband and I had a perfect view from our back window of the baseball field at an elementary school. In the distance, I saw three girls around 14 years old. They each wore what looked like a new bright sweatshirt and pants they may have just gotten for Christmas. Some boys in raggedy clothes walked up to them with a football. Reluctant at first, the girls joined them. The boys led them 100 feet away to where they were to play … in the mud. How the game went didn't matter, getting the girls muddy did. What the boys said to convince them I don't know, but I do know the outcome was mud from head to toe. Though they appeared to have fun during the game, afterwards, the girls looked ashamed.

We can assume the girls knew they had disobeyed their parents and likely delivered a heartfelt apology. Similarly, when we Christians know we have sinned in disobedience to God, we repent. God symbolically pulls us from the mud. Next, He cleanses us spiritually from our sins instantaneously and with much less effort than those girls went through to physically remove the mud. Sounds great! However, we must do our part by repenting properly. How?

- We don't repent solely to clear our conscience, but we recognize we have disobeyed God, a serious matter.
- Our words aren't just an intellectual acknowledgement, but from our broken heart.
- Repentance is a change in heart that leads to a change in behavior. We figure out how we could have escaped the temptation so we can try to apply it next time.
- Be humble. Don't make excuses or blame others. The girls could have blamed the boys, but it was their fault for not resisting temptation.
- Our loving God may discipline us. Accept it.

 When we repent sincerely, God heals the wounds of our sin.

39. POCO'S HIDING PLACE
Ways We Hide Our Sin

O God, You know my foolishness;
And my sins are not hidden from You.
PSALM 69:5

A white Chihuahua named Poco became part of our
family when I was 5 years old. He was such a cute
puppy who fit in the palm of my hand. As Poco grew
and wandered around the house, he found a hiding place
under the couch. Every time Poco got into trouble, he
scurried to his hiding place and stayed until he felt it was
safe to come out. It was a hiding place to Poco, but we
could easily see him. When our eyes met, the look in his
deep brown sorrowful eyes said, "I know I did wrong,
but I am scared to face you about what I did."
Eventually, out of his hiding place and with his tail
between his legs, he was ready to receive punishment
followed by a hug later. One day when Poco had gotten
himself into trouble, we watched him run toward his
hiding place. This time, it didn't go well for him. He had
grown so much he no longer fit under the couch. We
laughed at him and cried for him at the same time.

When Poco did wrong and hid, he believed that
because nothing could get to him, he was safe. Similarly,
we can try to hide our sin from God instead of repenting.
Rather than physically hiding our sin, we go through
mental exercises such as convincing ourselves what we
did wasn't a sin or that other good acts made up for it.
Doing this can seem safer than facing God. However,

rather than innocence and the safeness we had hoped for, we feel guilty and vulnerable. Our deception can cause depression, a feeling of separation from God, and a fall deeper into sin. Comparable to seeing Poco in his physical hiding place, God sees us in our spiritual hiding place because He knows exactly what we do and what we are thinking. Trying to hide our sin is foolhardy since we have an all-knowing and infinitely forgiving God who loves us and welcomes repentance.

 While hiding sin brings trouble, God's certain forgiveness when we repent brings harmony and peace.

40. REPAIRING THE DRYWALL CRACKS
Ways We Cover Our Sin

He who covers his sins will not prosper,
But whoever confesses and
forsakes them will have mercy.
PROVERBS 28:13

My husband and I did many of our own house repairs.
One such repair was drywall cracks, a task I mastered
over the years. I used different techniques to repair the
cracks depending on their size. After the repair, I applied
the repair compound and carefully sanded it flat. I
applied texturing to match the adjacent area. The paint
color matched perfectly. My methodical brush strokes
minimized their visibility. When finished, it looked
fantastic and there was no sign of the crack underneath.

What if I had skipped the step of repairing the crack
and just covered it with the repair compound, texturing,
and paint? It would have looked great at first, but it
wouldn't have taken long for problematic cracks to
appear through my covering. We can have a similar
outcome when we try to cover our sin. Ways we do that
and why our cover is faulty are when we:

- Pretend it didn't happen and move forward.
  Faulty: This isn't how God or Christians deal with
  sin.
- Keep it to ourselves by not telling others. Faulty:
  God knows all that happens.

- We convince ourselves that we can lower God's standard so that it appears we are not sinning. Faulty: God's standards are eternal and can't be changed.
- Justify our actions with excuses. Faulty: There is no excuse for sin.
- Do good acts to make up for our bad sinful act, so it doesn't count. Faulty: Good acts don't make up for the bad sinful ones.
- Compare it to something worse, so it isn't that bad. Faulty: Sin is sin, no matter how small.

Covering our sin is futile as it is still there. Sin hinders our fellowship with God. We won't experience God's blessings. Instead, we need to deal with our sin by humbling ourselves and repenting to God. In return, our gracious God forgives completely. In my example of the damaged wall, it would be like instantaneously replacing the drywall. That doesn't mean we are done. If our sin harmed others, we must make restitution. Also, with God's help in prayer, we come up with ways to avoid future sin.

 When we are free from the burden of sin, we will walk with God in joy and peace.

41. ROARING LION TURNED TO GENTLE LAMB ON THE PHONE
Reasons We Sin That Are Lies

If we say that we have no sin,
we deceive ourselves, and the truth is not in us.
1 JOHN 1:8

My life depends on ventilator supplies I order every four weeks. When the company I ordered them from didn't supply what I needed and gave conflicting answers over several lengthy phone calls, I expressed my anger at the customer service representatives. After years of doing this, I realized it was a sin. I prayed to God for forgiveness and to change my heart to be patient and kind. Also, I prayed before and after each phone call. Over time, I overcame my anger issue and didn't need to pray about it anymore. I turned from a roaring lion to a gentle lamb.

If I had not recognized my sin, I would have remained a roaring lion. Below are reasons we come up with to justify sin that sound convincing but are lies. To move forward, we must recognize the truth that explains why our reasons aren't valid.

- It is okay to take out our frustrations on other people (my reason). Truth: We can submit to the Holy Spirit and allow Him to produce the fruit of the Spirit* in us (patience and kindness for my case).
- It wasn't my fault. Truth: We are responsible for our thoughts and actions.

- Peer pressure. Truth: We can resist with God's help.
- Everyone else is doing it. Truth: As Christians, we follow higher standards.
- Sinful behavior isn't a big deal, and it is commonplace. Truth: Every sin matters to God and is serious.
- I can do what I want because God will forgive me. Truth: This isn't true repentance.
- Doing as I wish is my right. Truth: Our sovereign God's ways are best, so we obey Him.
- It has never harmed me. Truth: Sin will harm us spiritually.

Instead of an invalid reason that won't work, we are to admit the truth and our sin. If we don't, it is as if we say we have no sin. We are deceiving ourselves. The sin is still there and will fester. We claim to be in the light, but we are in the darkness. Because we can't be in the light and darkness at the same time, we are separated from God's fellowship. We are miserable. When we repent from our heart, we receive God's grace. Peace and joy return.

 Rather than tripping on our lies about our sin, we seek God's forgiveness and walk uprightly with Him.

*Fruit of the Spirit is love, joy, peace, longsuffering (patience), kindness, goodness, faithfulness, gentleness, and self-control.

42. POCO'S ESCAPES
Resisting the Lure of Sin

Evil pursues sinners,
But to the righteous, good shall be repaid.
PROVERBS 13:21

Throughout much of my childhood, we had a Chihuahua dog named Poco. He had a great life with endless food and water, a comfortable house, a loving family, play time, and quiet time with petting. None of these necessities and luxuries were outside his house and yard. Poco knew what was in the neighborhood from his frequent walks on a leash. Figuring it would be fun to explore on his own, when we let him into the backyard to relieve himself, he first checked to see if someone accidently left a gate ajar so he could escape. When he got out, I knew where to find him. When I did, he was often stressed. Sometimes, the grass that had looked so inviting was wet and soaked his legs and belly. He hated that. One time, Poco got a black stripe down his white back. Punishment for his escape had always been a tap on his behind. That time it included a bath which he despised. There was another outing when a car almost hit him. None of these negative experiences deterred Poco from future escapes.

Poco's experiences have many parallels to ours as Christians. Poco's family supplied his needs; God supplies our needs. Poco wanted the freedom to explore new territories on his own even though it was dangerous to leave the protection of his family; sometimes we think it would be fun to explore new experiences even though God warns us to leave them alone. Poco didn't resist his impulses; sometimes we don't resist ours. Separation happens. For Poco it was from his loving family; for us it is from God's fellowship. Poco's experience was unpleasant; for us so is living in sin. I knew where to find Poco and brought him home; God knows when we sin and will restore our fellowship with Him when we repent. I disciplined Poco for escaping; God can discipline us for sinning. It didn't stop Poco; it doesn't always stop us. What a perilous path of darkness! Unlike Poco, we Christians can resist it and take the path of righteousness by praying for God's strength to resist sinning. Additionally, we can rely on God and fellow Christians to help us renew our minds to godly thoughts and ways rather than conforming to this sinful world.

 The best place to walk is in the light of our righteous God.

43. THE BALL AND CHAIN
Unlocking Constraints of Sin

Now if I do what I will not to do,
it is no longer I who do it,
but sin that dwells in me.
ROMANS 7:20

In anticipation of a bachelor party, men at my office had fun with a torturous tradition. They attached a ball and chain to the bachelor's ankle. There was no escape as they locked it with a key. It was to jokingly signify that his new life as a married man would take away the freedom he currently had. Starting a family would rob him of even more freedom. The bachelor got many laughs when he dared to leave his desk, which he seldom did. Because every step he took was a lot of effort, coworkers helped him throughout the day. He was relieved when they removed the ball and chain at the end of the workday.

No one would want to wear a ball and chain. Yet sin can influence our lives similarly by holding us back, making life more difficult, or making it necessary to ask for help. These can affect us and those around us physically, emotionally, or spiritually. We find that our old sin nature causes us to do what our new nature in Christ doesn't desire us to do. Sin can be quite devastating in many ways by:

- Adversely affecting our feelings.
- Resulting in harmful vices, harmful habits, and bad choices.
- Taking our time away from God.
- Robbing us of God's peace, hope, and joy.

Thankfully, we have hope as God can unlock the constraints of sin. How? First, we humble ourselves and acknowledge we want to do something about it. Next, we repent, ask God for forgiveness, and He will set us free. That is all there is to it. However, this can be difficult for some sins. We may not want to admit them. They can be deep-rooted. Since it took a while for the sin to get there, it can take time to be free of it. For these more difficult ones, additionally we need to pray and ask God to reveal His plan to us. Whatever we do, God will be by our side to help us. It can be a lengthy process that is worth pursuing. I know as I have done it many times.

 Freedom from the power of sin makes life so much easier.

44. DIVING WITH FROG LEGS
Spiritual Constraints Ensnare Us with Sin

Therefore we also, since we are surrounded by so great a cloud of witnesses, let us lay aside every weight, and the sin which so easily ensnares us, and let us run with endurance the race that is set before us,
HEBREWS 12:1

At my cousin's house, I learned to swim proficiently in their large swimming pool. However, my diving form was terrible with my legs spread apart instead of together. People jokingly called it frog legs. In junior high, my teacher wanted me to correct it. Certainly, I could do that. Troubleshooting at my cousin's house showed that I started kicking when my hands hit the water. To break the bad habit, adults tied a band around my ankles. No frog legs! However, after I dove into the water, with my legs constrained I couldn't kick. That meant I could hardly swim. I bobbed up and down trying to make it to the safety of the edge of the pool. At first people laughed. Then when they realized the difficulty I was having, they got concerned. Finally, with no more energy left, I made it. We surrendered and decided I would have frog legs when I dove.

The band constrained my legs physically. As Christians, we have traits that constrain us spiritually. They weigh us down hindering our walk with God and ensnare us with sin. They include our:

- Comfort zone that we don't want to leave. Staying there prevents us from sharing the gospel.

- Habits that take away time with God.
- Pride that convinces us we are doing fine and don't need help from God or others.
- Sinful nature that we give into.
- Personality traits that are opposite of being Christlike.

To remove our constraints, we pray to God to help us figure out our shortcomings and make changes to overcome them. With our constraints removed, we can run the race that God has set before us. We more readily share the gospel, spend more time with God, have a better life getting help we need, make righteous decisions, and submit to the Holy Spirit as He develops the fruit of the Spirit* in us.

 Who would want to keep their constraints when it is so much easier without them?

*Fruit of the Spirit is love, joy, peace, longsuffering (patience), kindness, goodness, faithfulness, gentleness, self-control.

45. PITCHING HORSESHOES
With Practice We Improve at Living Righteously

He who says he abides in Him
ought himself also to walk just as He walked.
1 JOHN 2:6

At family gatherings, we looked forward to pitching horseshoes. The game is simple with each player pitching two horseshoes at a pole protruding 15 inches from the ground and 40 feet away. The players try to get the horseshoes as close to the pole as possible. A horseshoe around the pole is a ringer. One time, after my dad and uncle finished playing, they came in the house to wash up. We asked my dad, "How did you get so much dirt on your forehead?" My uncle explained, "When he missed, he said, 'Oops, I missed.' and out of frustration tapped his forehead with the palm of his dirty hand." This was a gesture my dad often used when he made a mistake. My uncle never told my dad he was getting his face dirty or stopped him from doing it. We all got a good laugh.

Pitching horseshoes was easy to learn but difficult to master. Similarly, when we want to obediently follow Jesus, it is easy to learn what He did by studying the Bible but difficult to follow His perfect example. Of course, this doesn't include miracles Jesus performed to show His deity, but other acts Jesus did to live righteously. While aspiring to live this way isn't a game, we can compare it to horseshoes. Like my dad missing at horseshoes, we miss the goal when we sin. My dad came up with ways to do better; we repent and come up with ways to avoid temptation to sin so we will live righteously. With practice, just like horseshoes, we will get better at living righteously. Bystanders cheer horseshoe players. Only Christians will understand our desire to follow Jesus' examples and give us support, guidance, and encouragement. My dad wore his mistakes on his dirty forehead. Our mistakes may not be obvious and only known to us in our conscience and to God. That puts the responsibility on us to recognize our shortcomings. Doing well at horseshoes makes people happy. When we live righteously, we bear fruit and God will shower us with blessings.

 Rewards far outweigh struggles when we succeed in life by walking as Jesus did.

SECTION 5
GOOD AND EVIL
INFLUENCES

46. ON ALERT FOR A BEAR ATTACK

On Alert for Satan's Spiritual Attack

Be sober, be vigilant;
because your adversary the devil walks about like a
roaring lion, seeking whom he may devour.
1 PETER 5:8

In Canada, my husband, Ed, and I stopped at a remote campground where there were no other people. We noted bear tracks next to the pit toilet. It was too late to go to a different campground. So, when we used the pit toilet, we carried a rifle and stood guard for each other. At night, Ed placed one rifle facing below our feet and a second rifle facing above our heads. Ed stayed up until four o'clock in the morning on alert for any sign of bears. Needing sleep, he asked me to stay awake and alert. I agreed. Not long after that, Ed begged, "Wake up!" I had fallen asleep.

Ed was a faithful guard, but on my watch, we would have had a much different outcome if a bear had attacked. As Christians, we must be vigilant on our watch against another enemy, Satan, who attacks spiritually and is much more powerful than a bear. One way Satan attacks is to paralyze us spiritually by terrorizing and intimidating us. Weapons Satan tries to use against us and how we respond include:

- *DISCOURAGEMENT.* Satan tries to cause us to become discouraged when serving God or following God's will. Our response: Don't give up. Remind ourselves it won't always be easy, but we can move forward through Christ who strengthens us.
- *SABOTAGE.* Satan tries to interfere with our efforts to serve God. Our response: Be thankful that "…greater is He who is in you than he who is in the world" (1 John 4:4b).
- *DOUBT.* Satan wants us to lose confidence in God's word. Our response: Resist Satan and remember that God carried through with everything He said in the Bible.
- *TEMPTATION.* Satan tries to lure us to satisfy the flesh. Our response: God gives us a way to escape.
- *OBSTACLES.* Satan tries to distract us from serving God, fellowshipping with Christians, attending church faithfully, praying, or studying the word. Our response: Pray to God to show us ways to overcome the distractions.

 God gives us the means to succeed when Satan attacks.

47. THE BALANCE BEAM
Spiritual Steps Take Us into Good or Evil

See then that you walk circumspectly, not as fools but as wise, redeeming the time, because the days are evil.
EPHESIANS 5:15-16

In junior high, the curriculum of gym class meant rotating through sports. One of my least favorites was gymnastics, though I enjoyed watching gymnasts on television and gained an appreciation for the skill they had. This class was where I got my first experience at walking on a 4-inch-wide balance beam. We started with one that was only a few inches off the ground, then one 18 inches high, and finally over 4 feet tall. To walk on the beam, I had to take care with every step I took. Gratefully, there was a thick mat under all the beams as losing my balance caused me to step off the beams many times. With determination, I learned to stay on the beam longer.

When I walked on the balance beam, I had to pay attention to every physical step I took. Similarly, in life's decisions, we need to pay attention to our spiritual steps that can take us in the direction of good or evil. As Christians, we are not to walk as fools following evil, but as wise following good. We do this by living righteously and staying in God's will. This is the best way to live, and it pleases God. However, when we expose ourselves to evil, we can become desensitized to it, blurring the line between good and evil, making it easier to inadvertently slip into the direction of evil. To follow God's good ways, we work at learning God's word and using its teachings to evaluate our daily decisions and habits and determine who we hang out with. Just like the balance beam, over time, we get better at staying where we should in the direction of good. When we slip into the direction of evil and sin, we can repent and get back up. When we struggle, God will help us. Living righteously not only furthers our walk with God, but we can also show God's light to others in what little time we have on earth.

 Time is a precious commodity to spend wisely.

48. CLOUDS BLOCK PHYSICAL LIGHT OF THE SUN
How We Block God's Spiritual Light

Draw near to God and He will draw near to you.
Cleanse your hands, you sinners;
and purify your hearts, you double-minded.
JAMES 4:8

Cloudy days were common where my husband and I lived in Washington. Many days were a combination of clouds and sunshine. Other days, we merely got a sun break when the clouds moved only briefly to reveal the sun. Some days, we saw no sun. One winter, it had been an extraordinarily long time since we had experienced sunshine or even a sun break. At my office, the clouds finally moved out of the way at just the right time for us to see bright sunshine. When it happened, several of us got up from our desks, walked to the window, looked out, and said, "The sun!" We just stood there and enjoyed it for a while next to our supervisor who understood our need.

While the sun gives us physical light, God offers spiritual light of the truth of God's word. Separated from God, an unbeliever is blinded to it. When God opens the believers' eyes, they can see it. Both light sources guide us in separate ways and are always there. We need both. However, like the clouds blocked the sun, we can block God's light by:

- distractions that prevent us from drawing near to God,

- indecisiveness between the lure of our evil flesh in the world of darkness and obeying God, and
- unrepentant sin.

Gratefully, we aren't in complete darkness like an unbeliever as nothing can separate us from the love of God. However, these rob us of our fellowship with God, so like a cloudy day, we can't get full benefit from God's light. When we block it, just as my coworkers and I missed the sun, we miss God's light. However, unlike our inability to control clouds that block the sun, we can stop blocking God's light. To clear the issues that block it, we put away our distractions to draw near to God, choose God's path of righteousness, or repent of our sin. In response, God will draw near to us, welcome our focus on Him, and forgive and restore us.

 How refreshing when God's glorious light shines on us.

49. THE PARROTS
The Wise Research What They Hear

The simple believes every word,
But the prudent considers well his steps.
PROVERBS 14:15

Pet parrots gave my husband, Ed, and me some funny moments by repeating sounds. I will share two such stories. Ed went outside through a door the parrots couldn't see from their cages. When Ed suddenly appeared in the backyard, the parrots squawked incessantly and loudly. I had to figure out a way to put a stop to that. To reassure them Ed was harmless and allowed to be there, I said repeatedly in a gentle voice, "Hi, Ed." That quieted them down. After doing this a few times, the parrots saw Ed in the backyard and, without prompting, responded in an imitation of my voice with, "Hi, Ed." On another occasion, we had kitchen chairs that squeaked when we swiveled. Ed said he would lubricate them. A few days later, Ed's chair still squeaked when he swiveled. I asked, "Didn't you lubricate the chair?" Ed looked at me puzzled and confirmed that he had. He swiveled again. The parrot had learned to imitate the sound of the squeaking chair when Ed swiveled in it.

Parrots just repeat what they hear without thoroughly understanding what it means. We can get in the lazy habit of doing that. This is never good, but it is especially dangerous when we believe what we are told about biblical teachings and don't confirm it. With an increasing number of false teachers, we can't trust everything we hear. What we can trust is the Bible. To ensure we keep our steps on the right track following God's ways, we research the Bible and its meaning by:

- Studying Scripture to understand the meaning.
- Using reliable study guides, commentaries, Bible dictionaries, and concordances.
- Meditating on the Scripture.
- Praying as we read, study, and meditate.
- Asking the Holy Spirit and mature Christians to help us understand the Scripture and its application.
- Considering how the Scripture applied when written.
- Pondering what God is trying to teach us.
- Preserving its meaning in its context.
- Keeping it as God's word by not adding to or taking away from it.

 The wise research what they hear to make certain it is true.

50. THE DESSERT IMPOSTERS
Evil Made to Look Like Good

But solid food belongs to those who are of full age,
that is, those who by reason of use have their
senses exercised to discern both good and evil.
HEBREWS 5:14

Competitors on television cooking shows can get quite creative. In one such competition, children made dessert imposters. They are sweet desserts that look like a savory dish. One example was a hamburger with bun, cheese, and lettuce. The buns were trimmed cakes with the perfect shade of frosting. Sesame seeds were chunks of rice cereal. The burger was a trimmed cake covered with chocolate frosting that had crumbled cake trimmings to give the appearance of a burger texture. The cheese was orange fondant rolled to a thickness of an eighth of an inch and trimmed to a seven-inch square. Lettuce was gummy candies rolled out, coated with sugar, and curled on the edges. When done, it looked like a savory burger with cheese and lettuce on a bun.

Just as the bakers made the sweet dessert look like a savory burger, evil can look like good in today's world. For instance, premarital sex leads to problems and is against God's word, yet television makes it seem normal with enjoyment and no bad outcomes. We can incur debt when we buy luxury items that are enticing but cost more than we can afford. Vanity and anorexia can plague teens who aspire to look like beautiful skinny models. Satan is a master at making evil look like good.

It is important for us to be able to tell the difference between good and evil by spiritual discernment. This comes from learning God's word, meditating on it, and praying. By knowing what good looks like, we will recognize evil. An analogy is that to learn to recognize a counterfeit bill, bankers don't study counterfeit bills because they constantly change. They study the real thing.

 To recognize evil, compare all things to God's word.

51. CURIOSITY OF A CHILD
Knowledge We Reap from the Bible

The heart of the prudent acquires knowledge,
And the ear of the wise seeks knowledge.
PROVERBS 18:15

Years ago, my mom and I regularly went to the park at the end of our street to walk her dog. I was quite a sight with a hose that went from the trach at my neck to the ventilator mounted on the back of my power chair. One day a little girl around 6 years old walked up to me. Her mom sat about 20 feet away. The worried look on the mom's face told me she was concerned about what her daughter would say about my hose. These types of questions didn't offend me. The little girl surprised us when she asked, "How does it feel to ride a bicycle with no pedals?" I laughed, then smiled, and explained how my power chair worked. A relaxed smile replaced the worried look on the mom's face.

Children are so curious they don't hesitate to ask strangers questions that can make their parents cringe. Their questions are usually well-intended and a way children learn. With the same curiosity, we should strive to seek the knowledge of God's word. If we still have questions, we can go to a mature Christian for help. They would be delighted to share their understanding of the Bible. Knowledge that we gain from the Bible benefits us in many ways.

- It tells us we need a Savior, Jesus Christ. This is the most vital fact we will ever learn, and trust in Him guarantees eternal life in heaven.
- It nourishes our soul.
- It shows us our sins so we can repent and return to God's fellowship.
- It instructs us how to pray to align our requests with God's will.
- It instructs us how to rely on God as our refuge and strength.
- It shows us what is important and what to focus on.
- It gives us a closer relationship with our loving Father.

Unlike worldly resources, we can be certain that the Bible is true. We learn from His word when we humble ourselves and are willing to learn and obey God's teachings.

 Even with sincere, childlike curiosity, we will never finish learning about our awesome God.

52. THE CHRISTMAS STOCKING
Don't Change God's Word

Do not add to His words,
Lest He rebuke you, and you be found a liar.
PROVERBS 30:6

As children, my mom, dad, brother, and I each had a Christmas stocking that was 6 by 14 inches. On Christmas morning, we looked forward not only to seeing what was in our stockings but also to opening the presents under the tree. When I was in my late teens and my brother in his early twenties, we suggested that we reduce Christmas gift giving. No longer trying to figure out what to buy for people who already had what they needed would make the season more enjoyable and less stressful. We all agreed to only get a couple of items for one another that would fit into the stockings. That worked fine for the first year for everyone…except my mom. The next year, she had good intentions, but she bought presents that were too big to fit into the stockings. Her solution was to tie ribbons from the stockings to each of the presents that she had placed on the floor. She decided that met the intent of the new rules because there were fewer presents. When she explained this to people, they complimented her on her ingenuity. Though my brother, dad, and I weren't happy about it, we went along with it for her sake.

My mom added to and changed the rules to satisfy her motives. Often changing rules to meet our intentions causes little or no harm. But this doesn't apply to changing God's word; it is never okay to do that. We do this by taking Scripture out of context, fabricating our idea of what God meant, or formulating our own interpretation. All of these change the meaning and God's intent. It can seem subtle when we do this, yet it is dangerous. Not only are we calling God a liar, but we are lying to ourselves. Doing this is a serious sin that can take us down evil and perilous paths. Also, especially if we don't recognize our sin and repent, God will discipline us. If following God's word as it is written doesn't fit what we want, rather than changing it, we can pray for God to help us obey or ask a mature Christian for advice.

 God's word is perfect and never needs changing.

53. EXPLORING ON VACATIONS
Ways We Explore the Bible

Open my eyes, that I may see
Wondrous things from Your law.
PSALM 119:18

My husband, Ed, and I enjoyed traveling along the
Oregon and Washington coasts. On one trip, we stopped
at every campground and vista of the ocean to know
what was there for future trips. Over the years, Ed
showed me many of his favorite places to camp and hike
that I wouldn't have been able to find on my own. I was
able to do that once by taking Ed to a place I had visited
as a teenager with my parents. Our goal was to find
breathtaking views, and to achieve this we took on the
challenge of steep and ambitious hikes. After studying
maps, we discovered many new hiking trails. Every time
we drove up the mountain from our favorite
campground, we eyed a trail that wasn't on the maps.
With switchbacks that zigzagged up a steep incline, we
figured it would offer fantastic views. One day, we went
on the trail. To our surprise, the top wasn't where we
expected it would be. When we finally reached the top,
our efforts rewarded us with a unique perspective we had
never seen. After many years of long and steep hikes, we
went on a small nature trail. It turned out that it also led
to breathtaking views comparable to what we had
worked so hard to find.

We can compare these experiences with exploring the
Bible in new ways. We can just read Scripture, which is

like going down a comfortable, familiar road, or we can do much more...we can "explore" it. New believers may need mature believers to help them get started exploring the Bible. Though studying Scripture can be arduous work, it is worth the climb with a new perspective that is breathtaking. Studying by listening to sermons and teaching, attending Bible studies, and using trusted commentaries, Bible dictionaries, concordances, and books will help guide our way. Favorite Scriptures become something we repeatedly visit to give us inspiration, glorify God, or help us through our trials. We can explore the Bible in new ways that take us further than we had ever experienced. Sometimes, gaining insight will be difficult and other times it will take little effort.

 God gives us wondrous insights, guidance, and teachings when we explore His word.

54. FOOLED BY FRAUD
Identifying False Teaching

To the law and to the testimony!
If they do not speak according to this word,
it is because there is no light in them.
ISAIAH 8:20

Fraud costs the global economy over five trillion dollars annually. We are vulnerable to fraud and must be careful when we answer the phone, open our door, visit our computer, go out in public, or sign paperwork. A close friend of mine just experienced this on his computer. A scammer stole his friend's email address. Thinking an email was from his friend rather than the scammer, the scammer tricked him out of $100. My friend was fortunate as it could have been much worse. He is quite smart and figured he would never be a victim of a scammer. Another friend had their identity stolen, an act that drastically affected her life. Many victims have lost their life's savings leaving them destitute. Eventually, the victim figures out they were deceived causing a myriad of emotions such as shock, anger, regret, embarrassment, anxiety, and depression.

Fraud concerns all of us. There is a type of scammer who should cause us the most concern, yet we hear little about them. They are especially dangerous in that we may never be aware they attacked. We may knowingly support and pay them. They can cause the worst damage to us even affecting our soul. Who are they? False biblical teachers. They have the perfect façade of the

Bible. They can know the Bible well, but don't love God or want to obey Him. By quoting Scripture with confidence, they can produce trust. Unfortunately, they deliberately misrepresent or water down Scripture so much they change its meaning. Their purpose is to tell people what they want to hear for their agenda, such as collecting money. They live in the darkness of evil. To defend ourselves, we study God's word, the truth, thoroughly so we can discern the validity of what we are hearing. If what a teacher tells us doesn't agree with God's word, they don't have the light of God in them. Of course, this doesn't apply to someone who unwittingly misinterprets the Bible. They willingly accept correction; false teachers don't.

 Shining the light of God's word into the darkness of false teaching will prevent us from stumbling.

55. ALWAYS HUNGRY
Spiritual Appetite and Hunger

My soul longs, yes, even faints
For the courts of the LORD;
My heart and my flesh cry out
for the living God.
PSALM 84:2

Because ALS affects my ability to swallow, I use a feeding tube to eat and drink. There are benefits to this. I eat more nutritiously than ever before with the liquid formula, cases of formula are delivered right to my home, and feeding is fast as each meal takes less than ten minutes. To spread out my meals, I eat four times a day with the last one at bedtime. Gratefully, I don't crave specific foods. Right after I started using the feeding tube, just like eating food by mouth, my body told me I needed to eat with hunger pangs when mealtime was approaching. After I ate, I felt full and satisfied. For an unknown reason, six months later I no longer felt full after I ate. For years, I have been hungry all the time, an unpleasant feeling.

We should always be hungry. This doesn't sound right, but it is. That's because I am referring to spiritual hunger, not physical hunger. Physical food fuels our bodies, but we also need nourishment for our soul. Our needs are for knowledge about God, to live righteously, to act Christlike, and to have a close relationship with God. Some ways that help us obtain these are:

- Studying and meditating on God's word.
- Praying.
- Fellowshipping.
- Listening to sermons, teaching, and Christian (Biblically based) music.
- Intentionally setting our minds on the Spirit rather than walking in the flesh.
- Repenting when we sin.

An appetite for food is good and natural, and a spiritual appetite means we are able to enjoy fellowship with God. Though hunger for food can be unpleasant, spiritual hunger is pleasant. After we physically eat a lot, we are full. Later, our appetite and hunger return, and we eat again. With God, it is the opposite in that the more of God we have, the more we want. We always have an appetite, are always hungry, are never full, and there is always room for more.

 God fills the hungry soul with goodness.

56. THE CONTAMINATED PART
Dealing with False Doctrine

A little leaven leavens the whole lump.
GALATIANS 5:9

At my job, one of my responsibilities was the engineering for cleaning processes performed in cleanrooms. The process ended with extremely clean parts. For one of the processes, the shop worker disassembled components, such as valves. They precleaned the parts and placed them in a basket. For final cleaning, they lowered the basket in a heated ultrasonic cleaning tank filled with a special cleaner. After leaving the basket in the tank for a specified time, they took a sample of the tank. If one tiny part was dirty when placed in the tank, it would contaminate the tank and all the parts, the sample would fail, and they would need to reclean all the parts.

Just as one dirty part contaminated the entire tank, when one person shares or teaches false doctrine, they start the spread of its evil. As people share with one another, the falsehood spreads. This happens because we are in a spiritual battle of good and evil. Satan's evil gains ground when we ignore its spread. Thankfully, God gives us the tools we need for this battle. We recognize false doctrine by comparing everything we hear or see to God's word. The Bible is always true and good. When a question arises, we seek the correct answer by praying, examining the Scriptures, consulting sound commentaries, and asking experienced Christians.

When we need help to stop the spread of false doctrine, we can pray to God and ask mature Christians. For the most difficult cases, we inform the church pastors or elders. It is their God-given responsibility to protect the church from false doctrine. They are commissioned and equipped to confront, evaluate, and correct the situation. Outside of our church, we can experience the spread of false doctrine from sources such as evangelists, sermons, lessons, broadcasts, publications, or social media. When that happens, though we can't stop or correct them, we can warn people of the false doctrine and share the truth of God's word. The further the evil of false doctrine spreads, the more difficult it will be to correct.

 Knowledge, discernment, wisdom, and courage from God will help us deal with false doctrine.

57. GAINING WISDOM AT MY JOB
Gaining God's Wisdom

If any of you lacks wisdom, let him ask of God,
who gives to all liberally and without reproach,
and it will be given to him.
JAMES 1:5

As an engineer at Mare Island Naval Shipyard,
management asked me to revise a 300-page document
that instructed workers how to clean and take gas
samples for piping systems. Since I had referred to this
document many times, I figured it would be easy. When
I read the instruction in more detail than ever before, I
realized that I didn't know much about it. Parts of it
were confusing. To gain an understanding, I asked
workers who used the instruction if I could come to their
shops and have them show me how they carried out
these procedures. To do this, I had to humble myself
because we engineers were supposed to tell them how to
do the processes, they weren't supposed to show an
engineer. They welcomed my presence and questions. In
years to come, I would ask lots more questions of many
and become an expert in this field developing processes
and writing documents used throughout the navy.

The workers didn't just give me knowledge. They
showed me how to apply what the instruction said and
gave insight not written down. That is wisdom. If we
only learn Scripture and don't apply its truths to our
lives, we will only gain knowledge. We gain wisdom by
asking God who will give it. There are similarities

between asking workers at the Shipyard for their know-how and asking God for wisdom.

- Just as I wanted to learn, we must want God's wisdom.
- Just as workers had wisdom I needed, God has wisdom we need.
- Just as I could trust the workers with their knowhow, even more so, we can trust God's perfect wisdom.
- Just as I humbled myself to gain the wisdom I needed at work, we must humble ourselves before God and realize we are not self-sufficient.
- Just as the workers welcomed my seeking wisdom, God welcomes us seeking His wisdom.
- Just as I succeeded at my job because of the wisdom I gained, we will succeed in life following God's wisdom.

 God has an infinite supply of His gems of wisdom for us to gather.

58. THE FLOWCHART
Follow God's Paths in Our Decisions

Direct my steps by Your word.
PSALM 119:133A

At my job, I made flowcharts to show the steps of processes. These flowcharts used primarily rectangles and diamonds. Words in rectangles described the process and diamonds had a yes/no question for decisions. Arrowed lines joined the shapes. As a practical example, a decision diamond on a flowchart asks, "Do I want to watch television?" A line with arrows from the diamond for a "yes" answer takes us to a rectangle that says, "Figure out what I want to watch and watch it." A line with arrows from another part of the diamond for a "no" answer takes us to another choice.

Imagine the size of mental flowcharts we use to make our countless daily decisions! For many decisions, we do what we want without much thought as described in the example flowchart. Doing this lacks a crucial aspect. The flowchart should have included whether what we want to watch goes against God's word, and if it does, to change to a proper choice. When we don't ask these types of questions, we might follow the lure of our sinful flesh to bring temporary happiness. Doing this routinely for trivial matters can make evil seem like it is okay. Becoming comfortable in evil can lead to following evil ways for more significant matters. This separates us from God's fellowship and can take us to dangerous places. To turn from sin and follow God's good way in righteousness, we acknowledge Him and follow His path according to His word. Even though we know taking God's path is right to do, we can sometimes have a tough time doing it because of our desire to follow our sinful flesh. With prayer, God enables us to be triumphant in turning away from sin. Over time, taking God's paths becomes easier and habitual. Our prior sinful desires diminish. God takes us on amazing paths we may not have even considered. With a closeness to God, we experience lasting joy and hope in our soul.

 Following God's paths on our decision-making flowchart takes us to the best places.

59. THE LOST KEYS
Staying in Touch with God

Let us draw near with a true heart
in full assurance of faith,
having our hearts sprinkled from an evil conscience
and our bodies washed with pure water.
HEBREWS 10:22

People often lose their car keys. That happened to a friend, John, who drove my husband and me to a secluded place in the forest. After an enjoyable hike, John felt in his empty pocket. Shock appeared on his face when his eyes went wide, and his jaw dropped. John exclaimed, "My keys! Where are they!" In panic, John walked around his car only to find all the doors locked. A peek through the closed window revealed the keys in the ignition. John expressed his frustration and embarrassment. He needed to get those keys back. Nothing else mattered at that moment. Aha! A cracked open backseat window. John stripped a branch from the forest to use as a long stick. There was hope. Exercising calmness and patience, John poked the stick through the window to unlock the door on the opposite side. After several attempts, he succeeded. John smiled and the worry on his face vanished.

Loss affects us physically and emotionally. Losing touch with God affects us not only in these ways, but also spiritually. Like any loss, we don't lose touch on purpose. In our busy world, we may not even realize it at first. When we become aware of it, reactions can be like that of other losses, but additionally, we will have an empty feeling like none other. The only being who is happy about it is Satan. While God is always there for us, some ways we can lose touch with Him are when we:

- Stop praying or reading the Bible.
- Let an earthly endeavor take our time away from God.
- Try to solve or handle our trial on our own rather than relying on God.
- Follow the evil ways of people we hang out with.
- Sin.

To figure out the problem and what we need to change, we approach God in prayer with faith from our heart, not with rote words, and repent. Forgiven, God restores us, and we have a clear conscience. We no longer feel empty.

 There is no better feeling than when we are in touch with God.

60. CROSS-STITCHED GIFTS SHARE ABOUT GOD
Reflecting God's Light

*"Let your light so shine before men, that they may see
your good works and glorify your Father in heaven."*
MATTHEW 5:16

When I lost the ability to cross-stitch beautiful works of
art because of my disease, I gave up on ever sewing
again. With prompting from an occupational therapist, I
figured out that I could do tiny projects. To sew
something worthwhile, I designed small patterns with
messages about God. Sewing large projects shifted to
small gifts with a deeper meaning. Giving away what I
make expanded from my friends and church elders and
deacons to people going through tough times. It is a
group effort with help from women at church who
distribute them. My hope is that it gives people a
reminder of our awesome God when they look at it.

We did this out of our love for God. When we behave
Christlike in what we do and how we act, people see our
good works that glorify God. Doing this is important
because we live in a dark world of evil ruled by Satan.
God is the source of the light of the world. As the moon
reflects the light of the sun, we reflect the glory of God.
This reflected light can further a believer's walk with
God or influence an unbeliever, although only God can
change the unbeliever's heart. Ways we reflect God's
light include sharing God's word, doing good works,
treating others with agape love, praising God, or sharing

how God has helped us in ways that went well beyond what we could have done. I think of these as gifts of light from God, and every gift is valuable and can reach many people in a variety of ways. For instance, while pastors' messages are vital to teach and guide many, a tiny message my cross-stitching displays at people's houses gives them a reminder of what God does for them. People may see reflected light when we don't expect it. That happened when an atheist friend once observed that the positive ways I cope with my trials and treat others was because I love God.

 Reflecting God's gift of light blesses many.

Other Books by Karen Sachs

Seeing Through My Outside. This is about how I became a Christian, my husband's diagnosis and death from cancer, getting my trach and feeding tube, conquering depression and fear by applying Scripture, and peace and hope with God. The book has many pictures of my husband and me.

Thriving as My Disease Takes Me Through the Valley of the Shadow of Death. This is about how I struggled with assistive devices and changed my attitude, coped instead of moped, lessons when my disease took me to dark places, the stages of grief, my will to live, and finding humor.

Life with My Shepherd: 60 Devotionals. These devotionals are about the Bible, prayer, trusting God, ways God helps us, being a doer of the word, reaching up to God, and trials. It includes a series of devotionals on Psalm 23:1-4 and James 1:2-4.

Made in the USA
Middletown, DE
12 November 2022